BRAND FACE®

Be the Face of Your Business & a Star in Your Industry

FOR HOME IMPROVEMENT PROFESSIONALS

Tonya Eberhart
Speaker. Author. Agent to Business Stars.

Ron Greenbaum
The Basement Doctor

BrandFace® (Be the Face of Your Business & a Star in Your Industry)
For Home Improvement Professionals
www.BrandFaceStar.com
Copyright© by Tonya Eberhart

Published by BrandFace®, LLC

Cover design by Stephanie Athas

ISBN-13: 978-0692679432

DEDICATION

Tonya's Dedication:

This book is dedicated to all those who believe strongly in their commitment to their profession. To those who believe that every person has a unique and intriguing story, and that their principles for success are built on their own story. To those who believe their reputation is their greatest asset, are willing to take risks and be fearless in the face of competitors. To those who are willing to become one with their brand.

Ron's Dedication:

I'd first like to dedicate these thoughts to my beloved wife, Terri. She's been my faithful companion in life for over 30 years, and has seen it all. From me being involved in the crazy ups and downs as a rock-n-roll promoter and manager, from being alone with young kids as I ran waterproofing sales appointments at all times of the day and night, to giving me the support while evolving into The Basement Doctor. Also to my extended family, I value them tremendously. And to our staff, they work in an ever-changing world, if it wasn't for their dedication, and the trust placed in me by our customers, I'd be in an empty building.

TABLE OF CONTENTS

Chapter 1:

INTRODUCTION TO STARDOM

In 1988, I was in Tallahassee, Florida attending theatre classes at Florida State University. I was also into my third year of selling Electrolux vacuum cleaners door to door to pay for college. Granted, it wasn't glamorous, but it was the best sales training I ever received, and is largely responsible for the publication of this book. One evening, I sold a vacuum to a radio station engineer and his wife. A few weeks later, the engineer called my apartment to ask if I was interested in interviewing for a sales position at the radio station where he worked. That interview kick-started my career in media sales, or as I often affectionately refer to it, show business.

It was while working at an AM urban station (WANM) in Tallahassee that I discovered what I believe to be one of the most impactful secrets of marketing. I noticed local business owners who had achieved almost a celebrity status, and I was eager to learn how they did it. I was fascinated with their local stardom, which seemed to elevate them both personally and professionally in their community. They were recognized in restaurants, at parades, sporting events, supermarkets and charity events. That familiarity carried with it an innate perception of positivity and trust.

What made these business owners stand out? They were the voice and face of their business, supported by a carefully crafted and focused marketing message. Their voices were heard regularly on radio, and their faces appeared on TV and in print ads.

Shortly after this realization, I began to carefully choose people from my own client roster whom I felt I could turn into the next radio star. I helped them to craft a message in their own words, one which could be delivered with genuine feeling and would also mean something significant to their customers. I underlined words and phrases on their radio scripts while hovering over them in the production room and, much to their dismay at times, forced them to re-cut multiple spots in pursuit of the perfect, simple message.

Since that time, I have counseled dozens of business owners and leaders to represent their brand, extending well beyond radio into TV, print, web, video, social media and more. When I started this journey, the internet was in its infancy, and achieving recognizable stardom through traditional media was both pricey and rare. The internet has proven to be a great equalizer. It provides more business owners and leaders the opportunity to represent their brand on more platforms. And with multiple devices being used at once (by the same person), all media types have the ability to influence the consumer, often beginning with traditional ad messaging combined with an online call to action. Once online, more opportunities arise for advertisers to interact with the consumer across multiple digital platforms, including related websites, social media platforms and search engines.

More platforms mean more opportunities to influence *your* consumer —but it also means more competitors with access to the same tools. It's more important than ever to reach the *right customer* with the *right message* at the *right time* through the *right platforms* with the goal of developing the *right relationships*. The success of all those efforts is held together by utilizing your appearance, personality and a strong belief system that represents your business across multiple platforms. Today's marketing choices are simply mind-boggling. This book was written to help you cut through the clutter and become the face of your business in a meaningful way that gets you noticed, elevates you as the expert in your field and keeps you in front of your core customers with unmatched loyalty and trust.

This book will help to ensure that your marketing and advertising investment is as efficient and effective as possible, featuring the one asset no other business has--YOU!

Ron's Message

A few years ago I was speaking at a local community college, and a student asked me a question which I've never forgotten. He asked, "Now that you're rich, why are you still working?" It really took me aback and I kept replaying it in my mind. While he thought there was a magical line I crossed and that I could now coast through life, I think myself and a lot of other entrepreneurs know that it's a constant effort to keep our organizations moving forward.

Let me share a little about my origins. I think it will help you better understand my frame of reference in life. For much of our young lives, my big brother Barney and I grew up as orphans, passed around 'the system' as free labor to whoever would take us. My mother passed away at a young age, and my dad was out of our lives. My grandmother did her best to take care of us while she could. We learned that if we were to make good things happen for ourselves, *we* had to make it happen. We had to find ways to help people in ways they appreciated. A solid future wouldn't be handed to us.

One of the pivotal moments in my young professional life came when I had a commissioned job selling suits. I quickly learned the value of the right way to communicate with customers. I was working with a man and began to say, "Do me a favor, try this on…" as I guided the process and in a helpful manner, let my customer know what he needed to do to get to the result he wanted. My job was to help him visualize it. I learned that a salesperson is like a tour guide, chaperoning the prospect through the options they have, and delivering at the solution they want. When done ethically and honestly, we arrive at the same place together. We teach this philosophy at our business today.

I've used lessons like that throughout my sales career and as The Basement Doctor. Our industry has a lot of unsavory characters in it. I've made it a cornerstone of our philosophy to be helpful, honest, and do what is right – by our customers, employees, vendors and communities. We've been practicing this culture since I've been The Basement Doctor, and held to it through all our growth phases. I refuse to use common scare tactics or a 'mark it up just to mark it down' sales gimmicks.

Thank you for taking the time to read about my *BrandFace* journey. It's an ever evolving process, but over the last several years I think we've really zeroed in on it. I hope you can use a few of the things I talk about to help you avoid the pitfalls and turbocharge your brand, marketing and sales teams.

Chapter 2:

BRANDFACE® FOR

HOME IMPROVEMENT
by Ron Greenbaum

The home improvement industry is certainly no stranger to the concept of personal branding. There are hundreds, perhaps thousands of business owners who are the face of their company. Many do well in their marketing endeavors, but there are very few who can achieve the #1 status—and stay there—which is truly the most difficult part.

For over 30 years now, we have been fortunate to maintain that #1 spot. As you'll no doubt learn throughout this book, there are many reasons for that. A business name that 'says what we are', a tagline that demonstrates 'what we do', brand consistency, superior customer service, incredible team leaders, top notch marketing…and much more. If you're a home improvement professional, you're about to learn many of those secrets to help you reach the top of your market. I would be less than sincere if I told you it could happen overnight. You can certainly get noticed quickly, but the brand that continuously proves its authenticity will be the last one standing.

We've seen many competitors come and go. I'm often asked for advice in dealing with competitors, whether they be strong and worthy, weak or even under-handed. My advice to you is to keep your nose to the grindstone and remember the goals, beliefs and culture that you set as your mission when you began your journey to the top.

I began my *BrandFace* journey with Tonya when my company just celebrated 25 years in business. We were already well established in our community, but we needed someone who could guide us to the next level. Change can be scary, but it is essential for growth. Tonya helped us to change our logo and create a new marketing strategy that has continued to serve us well today. Tonya Eberhart makes it easy to just read, listen, and learn.

I have been truly fortunate to live a 'Great Life', and I owe a lot to this industry. It is one of the reasons I am proud to offer my story and advice as the co-author of *BrandFace* for Home Improvement Professionals.

8

Chapter 3:

BRANDFACE® EXAMPLES

Let's take a look at a few nationally and regionally recognizable *BrandFace* examples. Many have stood the test of time, and some are so powerful that their impression and legacy stands strong even after their passing.

Harland Sanders, also known as Colonel Sanders, is the founder of Kentucky Fried Chicken. While operating a service station in Corbin, Kentucky, he began cooking for travelers. Since he didn't have a restaurant, customers ate from his own dining table inside the service station. He is best known for his 11 herbs and spices, his signature white suit, white hair and cane. His likeness still graces restaurant signs and millions of buckets in over 100 different countries around the world.

Dave Thomas started Wendy's (a fast food restaurant chain named after his daughter) after complaining that he couldn't find a good hamburger. His warm and relatable style as a spokesperson launched a hugely successful TV campaign for Wendy's. On the personal side, he was adopted at the age of six months, and his adoptive mother died when he was only five years old. Later in life, at the request of President George H. W. Bush, he began to speak out and encourage people to consider foster care and adoption. In 1992, he championed the cause further by starting the Dave Thomas Foundation for Adoption. Today, Dave's daughter, Wendy, continues his legacy as the spokesperson for both the restaurant chain and foundation.

Martha Stewart, an entrepreneur best known for cooking, entertaining and decorating, has written numerous books on those subjects. In 1991, she introduced her own magazine, *Martha Stewart Living*. Her growth continued with a TV show, radio show, syndicated newspaper column and a retail product line. Even after her conviction and prison sentence for insider trading, she continues as the face of her brand and her company continues to flourish.

Charles Schwab, founder of the Charles Schwab Corporation, helped to grow the company that bears his name to over 300 offices in the U.S. and one office or branch in Puerto Rico, London and Hong Kong. Though he left his position as CEO in 2008, he continues to be active in the organization and posts regularly as an authority on the company's *Schwab Talk Blog*.

Donald Trump is the hugely famous and sometimes controversial real estate developer and host of reality TV shows *The Apprentice* and *The Celebrity Apprentice*, to share just a few of his accomplishments. He is known for constructing and owning some of the most prestigious addresses, including Trump Tower and Taj Mahal. He's also known as a world class golf course developer. Though Trump's companies have filed bankruptcy four times over the years, he remains one of the wealthiest and most recognizable figures in the world.

Oprah Winfrey is best known for hosting her own talk show, *The Oprah Winfrey Show*, but her accomplishments include a production company, *Harpo Productions* (Harpo is her first name spelled backward) and cable television network *OWN* (Oprah Winfrey Network). Her philanthropic efforts are numerous, including Oprah's Angel Network, which has funded charities, one of which is a school for girls in South Africa. She became the first African American female billionaire in the United States in 2003.

Steve Jobs, often credited as a pioneer of the personal computer revolution, was the co-founder, chairman and CEO of Apple, Inc. He experienced a power struggle with his board of directors and was ousted from his own company in 1985. Eleven years later, his fame transcended those challenges when he returned to re-energize Apple, then near bankruptcy. His eccentric style and marketing savvy positioned Apple products as solutions versus products, making him one of the top technology icons even after his death in 2011.

Jillian Michaels, known for her role as the 'tough as nails' fitness trainer on the TV show *The Biggest Loser*, became a trainer as a result of low self-esteem issues and teenage weight gain. You'll see her face on magazines and in numerous digital ads as she promotes her own video workout series, clothing line, newsletter and books. She is one of America's most famous female experts in the fitness industry.

John Schnatter is the founder and CEO of Papa John's International, Inc. (aka Papa John's Pizza). When he was 22, he used some of the profit from the sale of his 1972 Camaro to purchase used pizza equipment and started serving pizzas from the broom closet of his father's tavern. Today, the company owns or franchises over 4200 restaurants in all 50 states and 35 countries. He is seen regularly in TV commercials during major sporting events.

Richard Branson dropped out of school at the age of 16, yet went on to launch Virgin Records in 1973. Today his Virgin Group holds more than 200 companies (including the recent Virgin Galactic, a space-tourism company) in more than 30 countries. He was the first to cross the Atlantic by hot air balloon and is known as one of the world's most colorful and adventurous entrepreneurs.

Orville Redenbacher grew up on a small corn farm in Indiana. He operated a successful fertilizer company, but never forgot his childhood obsession: creating the perfect popcorn. He dedicated all his free time to developing a new strain of popping corn, which at first was to be called Red-Bow. However, he was persuaded by an advertising agency to name it Orville Redenbacher Popcorn, and Orville himself represented the brand with his famous white hair and bowtie. He is known for his signature statement, "You'll like it better or my name isn't Orville Redenbacher."

James Dyson is a British Industrialist who developed the Dyson brand vacuum cleaner, a dual cyclone bagless system. After several initial failed attempts to launch his invention, he finally caught a break during a TV advertisement in which he claimed, "say goodbye to the bag", a slogan which stuck with his audiences and grew the popularity of the product. He went on to establish the *James Dyson Foundation* to inspire the next generation of design engineers.

Rachael Ray was working in a gourmet food shop in New York when she developed her signature *30 Minute Meals* classes, which were soon picked up by a local TV newscast. She has since written numerous cookbooks and has been the star of four different shows on Food Network, including *30 Minute Meals* and *Rachael Ray's Tasty Travels*. She launched her own magazine, *Every Day with Rachael Ray*, and shortly thereafter, partnered with Oprah Winfrey to debut *The Rachael Ray Show*.

Ron Trzinsky, owner of The Original Mattress Factory, decided to open his business in 1990, shortly after the mattress company he was working for was sold to investors in a leveraged buyout. He stars in his own TV and radio commercials and focuses on the quality of their construction, consumer product education and his company's desire to 'cut out the middle man' in order to save his customers money. He often encourages customers to tour his manufacturing facilities to learn more about their product. The Original Mattress Factory currently has locations in nine states.

Gary Vaynerchuk is an entrepreneur, investor, author and social media phenomenon. He operated seven lemonade stands when he was just eight years old, and became known for selling baseball cards at his local mall. In high school he joined the family business, a liquor store, and became obsessed with collecting wine. He founded Wine Library TV in 2006 and starred in the videos in order to share his passion about wine and to educate his customers. Soon, over 100,000 people were watching these videos. This strategy helped to turn a $3 million business into a $45 million business.

Chapter 4:

WHICH BRANDFACE® ARE YOU?

This book was written for business owners and leaders. You don't have to own your own business to become the face of a brand. A *BrandFace* can be a CEO, president, sales manager, salesperson, child of an owner, home-based business expert or anyone in a situation where they are likely to represent the brand for an extended period of time. Regardless of which position you hold, I've found that most *BrandFace* prospects fall into three different categories: *GameFace*, *SaveFace* and *AboutFace*. In order to get the most from this book, decide which description best applies to you and keep that in mind as you read. Knowing where you stand right now will help to prepare you for where you want to be!

GameFace:

Someone with a lot of confidence, a healthy ego. Their game face is always on. These people have no problem putting themselves out there because they strongly believe in the core idea that their business is built upon. Most have taken the personal and professional risks to build the business or brand, and are willing to openly express what they stand for.

SaveFace:

Someone with confidence, but who is hesitant to put themselves out there for fear of what others will think of them. They share the same characteristics as the *GameFace*, but tend to second guess themselves and their ability to represent their brand. They would rather save face than risk ridicule and failure.

AboutFace:

Someone who has never really thought about being the face of their brand and how impactful it could be for their business. I believe that people don't do business with a logo...they do business with a person. The *AboutFace* group just needs to be reminded of this, and after thinking it through are usually open to representing their brand.

-------------------- **Ron's Message** --------------------

My first taste of the personal branding approach came when Pete Scoville, a newscaster who interviewed me for Fox TV News, suggested I start doing my own infomercials. He was doing them for several others and said, "I do a lot of them for real doctors, especially dentists, and I think you'd be great at it". We met and he convinced me to try it, and that's when I started doing the commercials.

I'd definitely consider myself more of a GameFace, but from time to time the SaveFace has crept into my personality. Without question, I've always been comfortable in front of people. However, I was concerned from time to time that people would think I was egotistical since I was featured in all my advertising. I think we all have that insecurity deep down. However, I knew it was the right approach when we started it. I don't think I realized, however, the extent to which a BrandFace approach would affect both me and the company. It's made all the difference.

Chapter 5:

THE VERY FIRST STEP

Regardless of which *BrandFace* type you may be, the first step begins with *letting go*. You must let go of any intimidation or fear you may have about putting yourself out there. And yes, even those in the *GameFace* category will have some trepidation from time to time. One thing you must understand is that we are fallible human beings. We will make mistakes, and that's just life. Consider Donald Trump, who has been bankrupt more than once, yet continues to be respected for his knowledge and expertise in real estate and remains one of the most wealthy real estate developers in the world.

Let Go of Insecurities:
You're reading this book because you feel there's a chance that the *BrandFace* approach might take your business to the next level. You wouldn't have picked up the book if you didn't feel confident in your abilities and knowledge of your own business or industry. Embrace it. There will always be someone who knows more. But he who markets best, wins.

Let Go of Intimidation:
I'm sure you felt a little intimidated when you chose to start your business or begin a new career, right? We fall victim to our own intimidation at times, along with that of others who would question, mock or judge harshly your intentions to better your profession. Whether it's the fear of the unknown, fear that you won't have the time to commit or fear of what others think of you, lose it. Dr. Phil McGraw has one of my favorite quotes: "Your opinion of me is none of my business." Keep in mind that the negative opinions of others are often a result of their own insecurities and jealousy.

Let Go of the Follower Attitude:
Many times clients tell me, "I'm not sure I want my competitors to see my content. They will reap the rewards of my knowledge and steal my ideas!" This is what I call the follower attitude. You must let go of this fear of sharing knowledge. By extracting and unleashing your knowledge and expertise *first*, you therefore declare your competitors *followers*. Additionally, if your content is published, you have further proof that you were the original source. You'd be amazed at how intimidated your competitors will feel when you take the position of authority. You're a leader, not a follower. The confidence that instills will be very evident as you move throughout the process.

I chose to address these concerns in the beginning because 'letting go' is essential to becoming a successful *BrandFace*. You must have confidence in your decision. When asked by others why you chose to be the face of your business, you need to be prepared with your story. Know why it makes sense for you, and be ready to answer. To assist you, here are some suggested replies which demonstrate confidence, humility and humor. If it works for you, steal it! That's why I wrote it.

"Business is about risks, and putting my own image out there is a risk, too. But I believe in what my company stands for, and nobody tells that story better than me."

"Frankly, I almost didn't take this approach because I didn't want people to see me as egotistical. Then I realized—all business owners have egos and I might as well embrace it! It's either me or the other guy."

"I was really intimidated by this approach at first, but now that my face is out there, you wouldn't believe how encouraging people can be, even strangers. They tell me about their experience with our company and employees, and that they appreciate what we've done for them. I never really expected that response. It's humbling."

"Tonya made me do it." Yes, some of my clients actually use this one! Feel free to blame it on me when all else fails. Consider it my contribution to your risk.

Let Go of Worry:
What if something goes wrong? What if this is a mistake? What if I am not the right person to represent the brand? My answer to these questions is— who knows your business better than you? Who else is taking the risk to build your business, hire or manage employees and be accountable to your customers? Business is about risk, and you take those risks every day, regardless of whether your image is out there. You're passionate about your business and your reputation. Own it. As long as you carry that passion and commitment into everything you do to represent your brand, you'll minimize mistakes and set the tone for your employees and customers alike.

Finally, before you take the *BrandFace* leap, I cannot properly represent this concept without saying that being a *BrandFace* isn't for everyone. And it should only happen after careful consideration for your own personal needs and goals as well as the future of your business and any possible successors. I have often been questioned about the challenges and drawbacks, most especially the impact a 'changing of the guard' would have on a business should a *BrandFace* need to be replaced. I respond by reminding those who question that the most powerful and recognizable *BrandFace* in the world changes every four to eight years—the President of the United States—and yet we as Americans continue to hold the office in highest regard due to those in that *BrandFace* position who have upheld its values and ideals throughout history. The belief system and ideals of your business begin with you. But it ends with the legacy you leave behind. And that's the story *behind* the face.

Ron's Message

I received very positive feedback right away from this approach, so any fears I might have had were quickly erased. There is always a lot of recognition. People get very excited when they see me. They respond to me like I'm their best friend, approachable. I was waiting for someone at a restaurant the other day, and a gentleman recognized me and struck up a conversation. When we parted, he said, "You know what, you're a real human being. You really are who you depict in your commercials".

I'm the guy who gets out of his pickup truck and says, "Hey, how can I help you?" That completely removes any intimidation that might come with being recognized. What's unique about it is that I've become a Celeb-u-Brand (my own word for my BrandFace approach). It's when you are very active in the community while maintaining a consistent 'look and feel'—on top of being the 'face' of the company in your advertising. You become so recognized in a market that you actually become a local celebrity.

Chapter 6:

THE IMPORTANCE OF COMMITMENT

Over the years I've had the pleasure of working with some amazing business owners and leaders who are committed to being the face of their brand. Commitment cannot be over emphasized. In fact, I often tell new *BrandFace* prospects to think hard about whether they're ready for the work it takes to get to the level of local brand celebrity.

Allow me to take a moment to share my philosophy on commitment and why it's so important to any facet of a successful business. For almost five years I consulted media outlets on integrated marketing. I helped them develop ideas for their advertisers using traditional and digital media platforms to bring those ideas to life. I came from the media sales world myself, so I knew the biggest missing ingredients were fresh ideas and the ability to organize and execute those ideas to produce results for a client. If you ask almost any media sales professional today their opinion on the value of a great idea, they pay it great lip service. Unfortunately, it often stops there. Well executed, strategic campaigns are still largely missing in local and regional advertising today. Why? In my opinion, it's due to lack of commitment.

I spent five years consulting traditional media in an effort to help them bring integrated campaign ideas to their clients. Throughout that time, I learned that if I worked with ten salespeople on a staff, I'd be very lucky to find just one who would put into practice the principles necessary to achieve success. I believe that to be common, and as a friend of mine often reminds me about this subject, "That means huge opportunity for people like us". I also learned that if there isn't a commitment from the top down (in other words, management), success won't happen at peak levels. I grew weary of explaining to managers the importance of holding their sales staffs accountable to not only take our ideas and pitch them passionately, but to take advantage of the resources we brought to the table, and even to invest in their own education regarding integrated marketing. The lack of commitment at the management level of many of the media outlets we consulted is exactly why our company started phasing out most in that client category in 2011 and began consulting directly with business owners. At the time of this decision, we were still getting interest from media outlets, and still getting paid. So why would we move in a different direction? Aren't most consultants happy to have paying clients? My answer may surprise you.

I've always said that the most important thing in my career is my *reputation*. If I consult dozens of companies, but those companies are not producing enough success stories, how good is my reputation, really? *You're only as good as your last success.* I could have remained on the payroll of multiple media outlets who were not committed—or I could choose to focus on business owners who were passionate enough about their own beliefs, knowledge, employees and customers to grow their own reputations and create successes. I'd like to add that we still work with select media outlets by choice, but those are the ones who are truly committed. Since making that strategic decision, my own business has tripled. It was a big risk at the time. I remember lying awake many nights questioning whether this was the right approach. In the end, I remained committed to my own reputation.

So what kind of commitment would be required of you as a *BrandFace*? You'll learn more about this as you make your way through the book. Much of your time will be spent making strategic appearances in your community, conversing one on one with your customers and spending time with your staff to create systems and processes that ensure the level of quality you wish to deliver. With regard to your commitment to being the expert in your industry, most of your additional time will be spent extracting, organizing, developing and sharing content for your prospects, customers and peers.

Wikipedia defines content as "information and experiences that may provide value for an end-user or audience in specific contexts". If you are very knowledgeable in your field, you have a wealth of content in your brain that must come out if you are to brand yourself as an expert! I'm a firm believer that there will always be competitors in my field who know more and have more experience. But the difference between most of them and someone like me is the willingness and commitment to gather and share that knowledge in a teachable, meaningful way—to release insecurities and focus on helping someone else learn and grow.

As a potential *BrandFace*, you have experience and knowledge that few others can boast. The problem is—all that valuable information is in your head where no one else has access. And the only way you become an expert is to get it out and share it. At first, it seems a daunting task. After all, you've been hoarding all that knowledge since the inception of your career. So how do you get it all out? Depending upon the personality and preferences of my *BrandFace* clients, we have worked together to extract that knowledge from them in various ways, which you'll read more about in the Content Marketing chapter. Once we capture the knowledge, we make your content multi-purpose by utilizing it on your website, blog, social media platforms, printed books, e-books, white papers, e-newsletters, podcasts, articles, press releases, videos and more. And all of this feeds search engines with amazing expert advice from YOU.

I believe in handling expectations, so I want to be clear about the subject of commitment. Your commitment to learning and continuing to create great content from what you learn should never stop. The hardest work will be in the first year or two, as you extract and organize all the information you've either been keeping to yourself or sharing only with an elite group of individuals. It's a big job, but this book includes suggestions for taking those steps one at a time. It will be one of the most rewarding things you ever do.

I have worked with business owners who see this process as thoroughly enjoyable, because they are finally making progress toward becoming a sound authority in their industry, something many have dreamed of since beginning their professional journey. I've also worked with some who see it as a chore and just can't be bothered to dedicate the time. And if I may be so bold, those are the individuals who wasted their money—and my time.

Ron's Message

It takes more commitment than most people realize to be a *BrandFace*. I've spent over 30 years in this business, building the brand. One choice, one customer and one ad at a time. I think the hardest part of commitment is being consistent. From the slogan and jingle right down to the ball cap, we have never wavered.

The most important thing we do to commit to our brand is to consistently make sure that our customer service is above everyone else's. Our customer service philosophy is to listen, find out what they want to accomplish and then do our best to fulfill that list contractually and to the best of our ability. And yes, sometimes things go wrong. When that happens, the first thing we want to do is listen to their explanation of the problem, then we have to inspect and try to understand the full scope of it. We work arm in arm with the customer to understand the problem and tackle it together. We stick to what we agreed to as much as we can. Service is not a science, there's a bit of gray for sure. But when your name is on the business, you have to err on the side of the customer as much as possible. So, as long as their request is reasonable, we'll accommodate it.

Chapter 7:

TEN TRAITS OF A BRANDFACE®

These are the attributes I consider vital to the long term success of a *BrandFace*. I'm sure you've heard the saying, "It's much harder to *stay* number one than it is to get there". I believe there are a lot of people who can get there; some by hard work, others by sheer luck. But longevity is the key, and those who remain at the top demonstrate these 10 traits that I know to be present in almost every true *BrandFace* I have encountered.

1. **Dedication:**
   The confidence of every *BrandFace* starts with your knowledge and expertise in your respective field. This education requires discipline and dedication, exactly the qualities your competitors may lack.

2. **Equilibrium:**
   When you put yourself 'out there', your actions are on display everywhere you go. That means every decision you make, every action you take, could be witnessed by your community. Great *BrandFace* stars keep their cool and maintain balance. If they receive poor service at a restaurant, they remain courteous and respectful. They may never return to that restaurant, but they realize that one unsavory display of bad attitude on their part will last much longer than the taste of an over cooked filet.

3. **Generosity:**
   Every genuine *BrandFace* I've ever met is a generous soul. They give back to their community. They treat their employees and teammates with great respect and give credit to them consistently for their efforts. They are the first to reach out to those in need because they have likely experienced a need themselves in the past. With great success comes great responsibility, and they take it to heart. For this reason, this trait can also become a weakness when people take advantage.

4. **Loyalty:**
   The world is made up of powerful leaders and the loyal followers who support them because they believe in an ideal, a dream and the leader who carries that torch. However, you can't be a great leader without first demonstrating loyalty to those closest to you, those who help you achieve success. What you give, you get. Just as children

subconsciously long for discipline, followers long for someone to teach, inspire and motivate.

5. **Authenticity:**
    There are many *BrandFace* imposters out there, but those who live genuine lives at work and at home will persevere where others fall short. When they support a cause (while they realize the importance of sharing philanthropic efforts for marketing purposes) they do it because they truly care, not for the publicity. And sometimes they forgo the publicity because it's the right thing to do. Without this trait, a slick image or presentation is just a facade and the foundation a house of cards.

6. **Commitment:**
    I proclaim this as the number one trait that a *BrandFace* must demonstrate. Without commitment, you may achieve marginal success. But with true commitment, you will undoubtedly rise to become the authority in your industry. Time stands still for no man, but it's the one who realizes that the time taken to share and distribute your unique knowledge is time well spent in order to elevate your industry and rise to the top.

7. **Fearlessness:**
    I'm speaking of a specific type of fearlessness with regard to sharing knowledge. It's the ability to let go of the fear that a competitor will steal your knowledge and materials for their own advancement. The true *BrandFace* actually wants that to happen because imitation is the best form of flattery, and the original source of content is easily provable.

8. **Confidence:**
    I'm certain this trait is of no surprise to you. It takes great confidence to be the face of your brand. Ego is like power. It only becomes a negative if you allow it to consume you. My favorite definition of ego is 'the enduring and conscious element that knows experience'. In my opinion, confidence comes down to exactly that—experience. The more experience you have, the more confident you are in your authority and expertise.

9. **Care 'less' ness:**
    When you 'care less' about the negativity and jealousy of others regarding your *BrandFace* status, you have achieved a goal few others will in a lifetime. Many talented and knowledgeable people have

fallen prey to the negativity of others. It's imperative that we surround ourselves with people who will give us honest feedback, but from a place of inspiration and support.

10. **Responsibility:**

    With *BrandFace* status comes great responsibility. It means you are willing to live or die by your own sword. Putting your face, image and personality out there means that everything good or bad will fall at your feet and rest on your shoulders. When you are faced with questions laced with mockery regarding your marketing efforts, remind the one questioning you that you put yourself out there because you believe in everything your company stands for, and you're willing to take the fall should things go awry.

Ron's Message

25 Things I Believe

The following statements were adapted from a speech I made at Columbus State College for their Business Program's Leadership Speaker Series. Tonya watched a video of that 2009 speech and suggested we share these guidelines in a booklet called "25 Things I Believe—The Basement Doctor From The Ground Up", which was printed in February of 2014. They have guided me throughout my career as a business owner and entrepreneur, and I hope they are helpful to you in yours.

Kindest Regards,
Ron

1. **I believe CEO stands for Chief Education Officer**

   Training and coaching the people that work with you is the most important aspect of the business because you're only going to be as good as the people on your team. The front line of a company affects the bottom line. If everyone has the same vision, and has been trained to understand and do their job properly, you have a much better chance of being successful. Education is the principle responsibility, and it must start at the top.

2. **I believe you can't do it all yourself.**

   You need a team approach to anything that you do, especially if you are a service-oriented business or a business that relates to people. Teamwork is essential. In any aspect of a business, all members of your team must be rolling in the same direction. If that is not understood, then you aren't getting your point or vision across. Anyone in a leadership role has the responsibility of developing your team.

3. **I believe you should hire nice, honest, intelligent people.**
Businesses today are transparent; honesty is especially important. If you're not truthful, you'll find yourself on the internet. People like and want to do business with nice people. Sometimes just being nice is the difference between choosing your business over a competitor. Training programs are bountiful, but you have to have intelligence to absorb the training. The best employees actually train themselves. You want to find people who are hungry and passionate about what you do. If you can find people with those three ingredients, you have a good chance at success.

4. **I believe in using the word 'we' as much as possible when referring to our company.**
To be successful, people have to "buy in", COMPLETELY. Great leaders understand that it is a team effort. Every company is a group of individuals working together and striving toward the same vision and goals. The 3 keys to accomplishing this task are:
  1. They must understand the vision clearly
  2. They must take ownership in what they are doing and in the company
  3. They must be empowered and equipped to do so.

5. **I believe in taking risks—jumping off a cliff and growing your wings on the way down.**
It gets you into trouble sometimes, but most of the time, you'll find your wings. You have to take risks, and often they get bigger as the rewards get bigger. I have always had a lot of confidence that I can and will figure things out.

6. **I believe people deserve a second chance, but not usually a third.**
Giving people a second chance today can be tough. Most people are resistant to change. It has been my observation that people, when faced with stress or adversity, will revert to some pretty bad behavior and react to certain situations in the same manner even when the outcome is negative. When you are responsible for customer acquisition, revenue growth or the reputation of a company, you have to make sure that you have people that will do the right thing. It has been my observation that giving somebody a second chance is a coin toss at best.

7. **Confidence is one of your most important success ingredients.**
A big part of the recipe for success is confidence. I am a confident person, I always have been. Even at times when I am not self-assured, I always project that I am. When negotiating, you have to have that conviction to be successful.

8. **I believe in throwing people in the deep end to see if they can swim, but always have a life preserver ready.**
Everyone is hired with the expectation that they bring the necessary skill set to do the job. I'm going to give them initial responsibilities and see what they can do for me. However, I am always prepared to train them if they can't perform up to the level I expect.

9. **I believe in family, even though I grew up as an orphan.**
I think one key ingredient to my success and stability was marrying the right person and having a family. I think that is somewhat missing and often frowned upon in our society today. I am fortunate that my wife handled the responsibilities at home while I grew our business.

10. **I believe that in business, people are usually the problem and the solution.**
Hiring the right people is essential. If they don't share the same vision as their team members and the company, then you are going to have a problem. Don't struggle with someone who doesn't see your vision.

11. **I believe in hard work. Period.**
That's an easy one. Hard work is just that. Everybody's job description is really the same—any and all duties that are assigned. This means that whatever needs to be done gets done. An entrepreneur must work hard when they start a business. It requires a lot of time and effort, and sometimes physical energy. You can't get away from that. Every employee must have an entrepreneurial attitude. I've never met anyone who has a successful business who didn't work hard at it.

12. **I believe in enjoying life.**
If you're going to work hard and spend time working on your business, then it needs to be enjoyable for you. You have to find the joy in what you do, both at work and at play. Find something you are passionate about outside of work, too. I enjoy sports and playing golf; choose whatever it is that brings you joy. Otherwise, what's the point?

13. **I believe in the concept of rooting where you're planted.**
    In other words, don't have one eye on the want ads all the time. If you accept a position somewhere, stay there. When the going gets tough, a lot of people jump ship instead of looking in the mirror and asking, "What can I do to help or how can I communicate better?" The more rooted you are, and the more you understand, the greater the likelihood you will succeed.

14. **I believe everything is negotiable.**
    A lot of situations in life involve negotiation. Don't let your ego get in the way during negotiation. You have to be able to compromise and put yourself in the other person's shoes. Understand their circumstances and then think about how you can make it a win-win for both of you.

15. **I believe in written agreements, but I also believe your word is your bond.**
    You need to understand that once both parties decide on what they are agreeing to, it's not just about what's on a sheet of paper. You put it down on paper so that everyone can have an understanding of it, but ultimately, it's your interpretation. If you shake hands on it and agree to something, then stand by your word.

16. **I believe in women's intuition.**
    I believe my wife is usually right, except when she's wrong. That was kind of a joke, but that being said, having my wife as a sounding board has been very important to me. More times than not, her first feeling about someone we meet or an idea that I share with her, is usually correct.

17. **I believe in education, despite the fact that I am a college dropout.**
    As things are always changing in society, I believe that you have to educate yourself. It doesn't necessarily mean that you have to go to college, but it does mean that you must at least learn the basics. I think that there are certain people that benefit from a college education. I wasn't one of them, but I believe that over the years, I have earned many degrees just by reading, going to workshops, etc. and I think that's important. College may give you the book knowledge, but it doesn't necessarily give you the knowledge to be successful. I believe it is important to educate yourself, specifically in what you are passionate about.

18. **I believe in the philosophy that "This too shall pass".**
    I believe in living my life with the perspective that when faced with a seemingly insurmountable problem, there is always a solution. Even those

times when you think there's absolutely no way around it, I've found that thinking creatively and working hard usually provides the solution. And if not, it will pass soon enough.

19. **I believe in making profits, but not on the backs of my employees.**
Give credit where credit is due. You have to be sure to reward the people that work for you. You want to make a profit, but the profit can't be at the expense of the employees that helped you get to where you are. It's very important to have a structure in which people who help you and work for you are rewarded based on the performance that they give. That's usually pretty easy to do. Pay for performance.

20. **I believe in team leaders, not managers.**
I believe in providing training, but people should be assertive enough to train themselves. When an employee says, "I didn't get enough training," that's really just an excuse. If you don't feel you know enough, ask. If you'd like more experience, then create it. If you work for my company, I am going to ask you to solve problems, I'm going to ask you to save me money, and I'm going to ask you to negotiate. You have to find your own ways of solving these problems.

21. **I believe in myself and my ability to communicate.**
That's an important part of being a leader. You must be able to communicate because what you have to communicate is your vision. This doesn't just mean verbal communication. You must have the ability to communicate non-verbally. The essence of your business lies within your own thoughts and experiences, and no one can communicate that better than you.

22. **I believe I need to motivate people to do what they may not want to do, despite themselves, because it's in their best interest.**
Lots of times, people hit a wall. You have to motivate people by showing them where success comes from. There are aspects of everybody's jobs that they don't necessarily want to do. Motivate them by asking questions and encourage them to accept responsibility.

23. **I believe my biggest challenge as a business person today is to remove negativity, indecision and inactivity.**
You will never be able to get from point A to point B if you don't take risks and make business decisions. If you take one step backward, you have to take two steps forward to get ahead. If you never step back, you will never fall behind. Continuous, positive movement is crucial to success.

24. **I believe if you get new information, you can always make a new decision.**

You make decisions based on the facts that you have at hand. Much of the time, they're really not facts; they are just emotional sound bites. You may make a decision one day based on the economic or emotional climate, and if you stick by that decision just because your ego is involved, it could cause problems within your company. If you get some new information, you can't be afraid to change your mind. Make a new decision.

25. **I believe in giving back or paying it forward.**

Cause Marketing is an over-used cliché these days. The success of the Basement Doctor has been a joint effort between our team, our vendors and our customers. Therefore, as a business leader, I feel it's important to set an example of giving back to our community and our local charities. At the end of the day a business structure can exist, but it's the customers and the community that make a business successful.

Chapter 8:

BRANDING—

ARE YOU CREATING A FEELING?

A brand is the image or *feeling* a consumer has about a specific individual, company, product or service. This brand or feeling is created or manifested in everything you do, from your company logo to your tagline, presentation materials and company vehicles. For the purposes of this book, we'll look at *personal branding* as it relates to becoming the face of your business.

Personal branding is about defining yourself as an authority or leader in your industry. It's not all about how you promote yourself, but more about how you *conduct* yourself. It's about making sure that your own beliefs and ideals that your company was founded upon start with you and trickle down through your entire organization. Your personal brand is linked directly to the value your company provides to your public.

I strongly believe that people don't do business with a logo—they do business with a person. They love the story behind a brand, and they connect to that story and that individual. I also believe that every person already has a personal brand. They just may not have learned to communicate it yet.

Let's look at ways to communicate your own personal brand, and then we'll explore the branding elements that help to brand *you* and the brand you wish to achieve for your company.

BRANDING YOU
As a *BrandFace*, your company brand is really just an extension of your personal brand. Your job is to communicate what you stand for, why you insist on doing business the way you do and what that means in the lives of your customers. In order to communicate your brand in a way that evokes the feelings you want your customers to have, you need to plan for it. Here are some ideas which will help you put on your best *BrandFace*.

Personal Style:
One of my clients is well known for his signature blue and red baseball cap imprinted with his logo. He wears it everywhere, no matter the type of event. He has been successfully branding himself for over 25 years, and is by far number one in his industry and market. While a baseball cap might not be the right apparel for you, consider a signature style. That could encompass

being stylishly dressed everywhere you go, being seen as fashion forward. Consider shows like American Idol or The Voice, and how they style each contestant in order to have their look match their singing style or personality. Do you remember the signature fringed leather jacket worn by Gerry Spence, an attorney interviewed on cable news networks during the O.J. Simpson trial? He wrote a book called *The Making of a Country Lawyer*, which explains the country style of his jacket. It gives a laid back, casual appearance, one of approachability. And nothing says casual and approachable like the country. If you're not sure what your signature look should be, consider working with a stylist to help you discover that. It doesn't have to be drastic, nor does it need to center around one piece of apparel, but your personal image should be consistent with the impression you want to portray.

Personal Images:
When I work with clients to bring out their authentic image in marketing materials, we start with defining their style, then we schedule a photo shoot. By the time this takes place, I generally have a good idea of the personality I'm working with, and can suggest poses, which will be consistent with the image they wish to present. Hiring someone to do a professional photo shoot is one of the most important tasks on your *BrandFace* checklist. Don't hand this off to an amateur! Be sure to work with someone who will capture your authentic personality, your genuine smile and even your interaction with others. I've seen photos, which appear to be re-touched more than once, blurred for a softened effect and even glowing. Those are not genuine representations of anyone. Let your photos capture the real you. You'll find more detail in the Photo Shoot chapter.

Business Cards:
Your personal business cards should reflect your business philosophy as well as your personality. I like the use of photos on business cards because people tend to forget faces, especially after large networking events or after much time has passed since the initial meeting. Having your photo on your card can 'connect the face with the name'. If you're not comfortable with this option, consider a QR code, a barcode that can be scanned with a smartphone and linked to any online destination. Link your business card QR code to an introductory video about you and your company. The beauty of QR codes is that you can change what they link to at any time without changing the barcode itself. Even if the people who receive your card never scan the code, it brands you as technologically savvy, and that's never a bad thing.

Transportation:
Your personal source of transportation can be a signature of your brand as

well. Whether it's a hybrid vehicle, which represents your stance on the environment or a rugged 4-wheel drive to represent your outdoor adventures, it's another element that can extend your brand. If you don't mind driving a vehicle with your logo, it's not only a driving billboard, there is no mistaking the connection between you and your company. Every opportunity counts.

Signature Phrases:
Remember the Dos Equis campaign, with that signature phrase, "Stay thirsty, my friends?" Or "Campbell's Soup…Mm Mm Good." If you have a signature phrase that associates with your brand, use it in your blog posts, ads and speaking engagements.

BRANDING YOUR BUSINESS
Now that you have some ideas for your own personal branding, let's look at some branding elements to successfully brand your business with the same kind of consistency. Many factors make up a successful brand, like signature colors, logo, images, design elements and more. Decide what kind of overall image you want to portray to your customers. Is it an upscale image, Middle America, blue collar, intellectual, athletic, healthy? Which facets are most impactful for the impression you want to achieve?

Logo:
A logo is a business mark, which will be your companion on all your marketing materials, so choose it wisely. First, you must be able to clearly read the logo. A simple test is one I call the bumper sticker test. If you can clearly read it on the car in front of you, it's a great start. Of course, there are many other qualities of a great logo. For instance, simplicity. It's easy to include too many elements in a logo. Keeping it simple means it will be understood and recognizable on any size scale. Look at the simplicity of the 'I Love New York' logo, designed in 1975. Another thing to keep in mind is that your logo doesn't necessary need to say exactly what you do. Consider the Starbucks logo (a mermaid). You want to make sure the logo represents an extension of you *and* your company, from the colors to the font.

Tagline:
A great tagline is just as important as the logo. It really defines what your business does. One of my favorite taglines belongs to SERVPRO, a fire and water restoration company. Their tagline reads, "Like it never even happened". That says exactly what they want people to feel about their company. Taco Bell's "Think outside the Bun" is perfect, considering that their fast food competition is mostly burgers and sandwiches. When considering a tagline, think about the reason you started your business, the one-liner that will connect people to what you're all about.

Colors:

There is a lot of research behind colors and how they affect a brand. Restaurants choose certain colors, which have been shown to entice people to eat faster in order to turn tables for greater profit. Spas and salons choose soothing colors designed to relax their customers and encourage them to return. Sports franchises choose colors based on strength and aggressiveness. Do some research of your own to help you determine which colors will appropriately represent your brand.

Images:

Before we begin to create marketing materials for our *BrandFace* clients, we generally select two or three signature images which will represent the brand. Those images are repeated in backdrops behind your photos, in videos, as cover photos on social media outlets or as elements of print ad campaigns. Repeating a signature look through images creates consistency and eliminates the confusion that can occur when businesses use too many photos in their materials. Imagine if you saw a different background or image each time you viewed a company's video or saw their digital display ads? Too much variety can't possibly stick in the consumer's mind. Combining the right look with consistency is the key to a recognizable brand.

Design Elements:

A simple design element can provide excellent recall power for your brand. For instance, Nike uses the signature swoosh on all their products. And auto makers have signature emblems which are uniquely identifiable. Your design elements can be as simple as wavy lines, a sunburst or polka dots.

Sound:

You may have heard the term *sonic branding*. Sound can be a powerful part of your overall brand. What does your company *sound* like? This encompasses everything from your on-hold music to your jingle. You may be familiar with the five recognizable musical notes behind McDonald's 'I'm lovin' it' campaign, or the signature sound of Intel when you fire up your computer. And who can forget the infectious giggle of the Pillsbury Doughboy? Or the memorable melody of the Oscar Mayer Weiner song? Even singing or saying the name of your brand in an unusual way, like the quirky Yahoo! sound or the memorable, stretched first syllable of Ricola. Well-executed sonic brands can be more recognizable than the company's logo, and powerful enough to create and maintain the feel of a brand in mere seconds. I'm a big proponent of utilizing jingles in radio and TV commercials. I think it provides a deeper connection to the brand. One of my clients has been repeatedly approached over the years at local parades and other community events with people who desire nothing more than to sing his jingle in his presence and have their photo taken with him. That's when you know you've created a successful, memorable sonic brand! Here are what I consider to be the top qualities of a great jingle:

Sticky:
Just as it sounds, this means the song sticks in your head. Not just the melody, but the words. Even if you hate it, the fact that it's sticky can mean great marketing.

Relatable:
Do you understand and relate to the business because of the jingle? Does it make sense with what you know about the product or service? Consider the connection to what you provide and the problems you solve for your customers. Think about "break me off a piece of that Kit Kat bar." It perfectly connects with a specific characteristic of the candy bar, the fact that you break it off in sections to eat it.

Simple:
Keeping the words in your jingle very simple will ensure that the public understands every word. Have you ever heard a jingle that made you pause because you didn't understand all the words in it? That means you spent more time being perplexed about what the word could have been than associating it with the brand! Consider FreeCreditReport.com's jingle. Very simple lyrics tell a humorous story and end with the web address. Or Meow Mix's "Meow, meow, meow, meow" repeatable lyrics.

Rhyming:
The easiest lyrics to remember are those that rhyme. It's just the way the brain works. "The best part of waking up...is Folger's in your cup".

Harmony:
No, this isn't about actual harmonies. It's about making sure your sound is the perfect harmony between the feeling that best suits your brand and that with which your audience will best identify. Consider whether you want an upbeat sound, or more relaxed and laid back.

Your Business Name:
I'm shocked each time I hear a jingle without the business name in it, but it happens. I strongly believe that every jingle should have the

business name in the last stanza, so it's the last thing you hear. Consider "Stanley Steemer, your carpet cleaner" or "Frosted Lucky Charms, they're magically delicious!" Your jingle can be super creative and catchy, but if the public can't even recall your business name, you've defeated its entire purpose.

Ron's Message

Branding is my strong suit. And it all starts with the name. Originally, we were J&D Basement Systems. That name didn't carry with it any personality or even really say a lot about who we were. Then one day while I was traveling, I happened to see a billboard for the House Doctor, and I thought, that's what we do! We fix basements, just like a doctor. Immediately, I trademarked 'The Basement Doctor' in 48 states. Fast forward to today, and we're fighting off trademark infringements as a regular marketing function.

Once the ads started and I became the face of the Basement Doctor brand, part of my persona was the signature blue and red baseball cap. Frankly, the hat started with vanity. I was losing my hair, but I also wanted to protect myself from the sun. Then it just evolved. I noticed my brand wasn't entirely complete without it. Even in local articles written about me, they mentioned 'the guy in the ball cap'.

From there, everything we do is part of the brand. The way we answer our phones, the way we enter a home, our process and systems, our truck signage, our call center, all of it. The feeling we create with the brand is one of trust and credibility, and we've proven to be worthy in those areas over all these years and thousands of happy customers later.

Example A: The Basement Doctor Jingle
BrandFace examples can be found in this book starting on page 116

Chapter 9:

POSITIONING YOUR BRAND
FOR SUCCESS

Before you can begin to market yourself effectively and put your face on a brand and perception, you must define your point of differentiation. What is it that makes you or your business truly *different*? This is perhaps the most difficult step of marketing for many business owners and leaders. When I ask people about their market position, they often launch into a monologue about how they have better customer service, superior quality of products and services or have been around longer than their competitors. While that sounds reasonable to most, it's what *every* business owner states. And when everyone says the same thing, no one stands out.

Two of my favorite marketing books are *Positioning* and *The 22 Immutable Laws of Marketing*, both written by Al Reis and Jack Trout. In *22 Laws*, the Law of Leadership states, "It's better to be first than it is to be better". Therefore, staking your claim in your industry and market first is critical to the success of establishing a clear position for you and your business.

When choosing a position, think about the problems your process, products or services solve, and how you deliver that solution to the marketplace in a *different* way. If you're wondering whether you've chosen a position—or the *right* position, here are some categories and questions to help you discover what really makes you different.

Quality of Products:
What specifically makes your products better? Do they last longer? Are they more durable? Do they contain a special ingredient that no other product has? Are they simpler to install or assemble? Are they friendlier for the environment?

Type of Products:
Do you have a unique product or one that is new to the market? Do you carry a line of products that is exclusive to your business? Do you have a product that is sought after right now? One that celebrities are using? Does your product solve a problem your customers don't even know they have yet? Are they packaged in a more convenient or creative way?

Standard of Service:

Are your standards higher than your competitors—and provable? Do you have a quality control process that greatly minimizes errors? Do you have a checklist for your services that ensures peace of mind for your customers?

Type of Service:

Do you offer lifetime warranties that are unusual for your industry? Do you offer a service that is new or groundbreaking? Do you offer services that are a popular trend?

Customer Service:

This category goes well beyond a friendly voice on the phone. Do your employees remember all their customers by name? Do they write down your customer's preferences and remember them the next time they visit? Do you greet your customers with coffee or tea? Do you send a special gift to all your customers on their birthday? Do you go where your customers are instead of making them come to you? Do you send detailed information prior to an appointment to set your customer's expectations? Do you have a playground or nursery to occupy children while parents shop?

Someone Stole My Position! Now What?

So what do you do when someone has the *BrandFace* position you want? Again, according to Reis and Trout, the Law of Category says, "If you can't be first in a category, set up a new category you can be first in". If someone already owns the position you want, it will take too much energy to fight it, and you're beginning at a loss in the mind of the consumer. You want to be certain you own your position lock, stock and barrel. In order to be successful, this category must have two characteristics. It must be meaningful to your customer, and it must be authentic. Think about why your customers do business with you. What do you do extremely well that's also very important them?

Ron's Message

Our position is built upon delivering a 'Drier, Cleaner, Healthier, Safer, More Energy Efficient Home'. When we started our 'drumbeat', it was initially just one beat. A drier basement. Then we realized that every basement we tackled had some type of mold. Every time you have a water problem, you develop the byproducts. Mold was the industry's four-letter word. But we were very early adaptors in the industry to realize that mold needed to be addressed. Most other companies didn't want to address it due to the liabilities and legal aspects. But we educated ourselves and learned all that and how to cure it. Then our focus became a drier, cleaner and *healthier* home.

As we evolved into basement finishing, we added egress, which meant a *safer* home. Then we realized, "Hey, it's still cold down here". We became educated about the stack effect, where cooler air enters your home through the foundation. We learned the most technologically advanced ways to deal with all these things. Today, we're pioneers in the industry. In fact, if you see the ads from other industries, it's all focused on the overall health of your home.

We had been delivering that slogan for years in our advertising when I first met Tonya. One of the things she helped us with initially was a new logo and company tagline. I remember sitting in the conference room one day when she asked me to describe in one sentence exactly what we did. And I said, "Well, we fix all sorts of problems in basements and we finish them, too". She said, "From Fixed To Finished. That's what you do." I felt it was the perfect tagline and we ran with it.

Chapter 10:

HOW TO DO A
STAR PHOTO SHOOT

A photo shoot? Me? Professional photo shoots are not just for runway models. They're also a must for *BrandFace* candidates. Would you put sub-par products in your showroom? Or send sloppy salespeople to visit your customers? Obviously not. So putting *your* best face forward is just as important to your overall perception and business brand.

When I first bring up the topic of a photo shoot to a client, I sometimes see the 'rolling of the eyes' and even a client with a high level of confidence begins immediately to blush—at least until I explain the importance of this task.

Your face will appear on marketing materials and in TV spots, print ads, direct mail and digital ads. But we don't stop there. We add those same carefully produced images to social media platforms, email marketing messages, your website, blog, collateral materials and more. With all of these elements, it's critical to have multiple *quality* photo options to choose from.

Where do you start? First, embrace the concept and realize that your image is a huge part of your brand. Have fun with the photo shoot, and just be yourself. In addition, here are some great tips to keep in mind.

SHOOT GUIDELINES
Hire a professional:
Don't hire your niece, who just purchased a new pink Nikon to take prom pictures. I know. I'm harsh. But trust me, I've seen it happen. Do it right. You can get great quality photo sessions starting at about $500 from some excellent photographers. Ask other high profile business owners for referrals, or look through locally produced magazines that source their photographers.

Backdrop:
Shooting photos against a green screen or white backdrop will allow your graphic designer or photographer to isolate your image and crop out the background. This means that your image can be used with any type of background, which comes in very handy in many situations.

Top to Bottom:

Don't stop at headshots. Do close-ups, shoulders-up, and full body shots. Your photographer will drape the green or white backdrop down onto the floor for the full body shots so your entire image can be cropped from the background. An experienced photographer will also interview you in advance to determine the best poses and shots for what you wish to accomplish.

Use Props:

Bring a chair or even a table into the shot for a little variety. Both you and the chair can be cropped from the background and inserted into another image later. Using a chair gives a little informality to the shoot, and can produce some great photos. Take a few additional shots holding your main product offerings, too.

Change Outfits:

Bring three changes of clothing to your photo shoot. Two professional outfits (dress, suit, tie, etc.), one business casual and one casual, such as jeans. Of course, if you have a signature uniform, bring that along as well. These variations are helpful depending upon the use of the image and also the colors of the background on which your image appears. Some colors coordinate better with certain backgrounds.

Colors:

White or dark, bold colors photograph best for photo manipulation. Try to stay away from light pastels unless you are wearing a darker jacket over them. And no patterns, please! Stripes and floral patterns can be problematic. Finally, stay away from bright green, as it's difficult to crop out the green background without making you disappear as well. In fact, that's how many movie companies produce the 'invisible' shots—the actors wear the same color green as the background, which makes both the background and like colors disappear in the editing process.

No Cheese:

Is there a real estate agent in your market who still uses their Glamour Shots photo from 1986? A look that's either too polished, conservative or even too casual can make you appear unapproachable. Invite a friend to your photo shoot who makes you comfortable and can make you laugh. A genuine, friendly smile will warm the hearts of all your customers.

Promotional Shots:

Stage some poses for promotional use. Pose with your hands in the air signifying victory, or with your hands out as though you are holding a sign or a product. It may feel weird during the shoot, but we marketers can think of some creative things to do with those shots—like insert a sign introducing a new service, or place a product in your hand through the magic of image editing. In addition, hold a blank poster or sign, as well. Your graphic designer can superimpose the cover of your book, DVD or other promotional messages on top of the blank sign. Again, work with your photographer in advance to brainstorm some poses that represent your personality, your work and your specific marketing needs.

Engagement Shots:
No, I don't mean that kind of engagement. Show some photos of you doing what you do every day. Working on something, talking with your staff, holding a meeting, greeting customers, etc. These shots need to take place without the green or white backdrop, and can be a great option for collateral materials.

Go Candid:
In several of your photos, you will need to look directly into the camera with that warm smile. But candid shots are fantastic for marketing as well. They allow the public to see more sides of your personality. A good photographer will continue to snap shots between directing you through the different poses.

A professional photo shoot can elevate you and your brand. When you put your best face forward, it differentiates you from your competitors in a way that says you're professional, thoughtful and you care about your own image as well as the image of your company.

-------------------- **Ron's Message** --------------------

I get my photo taken at least twice a week with customers and fans alike, but I'm still not really used to seeing myself on camera. Although Tonya will tell you that I have dodged a full photo shoot longer than anyone she knows, I do realize the importance of having several different types of photos to use in our marketing materials. At some point, I'm sure I'll have to give in.

Example B: Sample photo shoot images

Chapter 11:

ALL ABOUT YOU!

When business leaders like you go about 'the business of running a business', you seldom think about things like bios and press kits. Who needs those anyway? Now *you* do, Mr. or Ms. *BrandFace*. It's a tough burden, but someone has to be a star. Bios and press kits are common in the speaking world, but many don't realize how helpful they can be beyond that purpose. When media outlets are seeking credible content, the presence of a compelling biography and professional press kit could be the thing which lands *you* the story or article instead of your competitors.

In addition, as you create content in various forms, one of those should be a book, whether it's a traditional printed book or an e-book. This makes you an *author*. Authors need bios and press kits. And authors get interviews and speaking engagements.

In the dedication for this book, I mentioned that every person has a unique and intriguing story. This is the place to share yours. Here are some guidelines to get you started.

YOUR BIOGRAPHY
You'll need a bio for more purposes than you may think. It will go on the *About* page of your website, as well as your *News* or *Media* page. You'll need a short version for the bottom of press releases and blog posts. If you publish a book, you'll need versions of it for the back cover and the last page of the book. You'll also use one in your social media profiles and as an introduction when you speak.

Several Lengths:
For all the reasons listed above, you'll need various lengths of your bio. Start with 50, 100, 250 and 500 word bios, and those should cover most occasions.

Write In Third Person:
Always write your bio in third person. It should sound as though it was written by someone who thinks you're the greatest business mind in the history of the world. Well, maybe that's a little dramatic, but it's a great starting point. If you are writing it, don't be shy. Pretend you're writing it about someone else, and it's your job to get them hired to speak at the next national TED Talks conference.

Opening Statement:
State your profession in the very first sentence. For example, my bio starts with "Tonya Eberhart is a speaker, author and agent to business stars". Right off the bat, readers know what I do.

Where You Live:
If you think about the conversation you have when you first meet someone, you usually end up discussing your hometown within minutes. It's one of the first means of finding common ground with others. Based on where we grew up or where we live, people draw conclusions about many things, good or bad. Instinctually, they will attempt to find something in common, though.

Professional Accomplishments:
Mention the founding of your business if you are the owner, or your position and purpose as a business leader, as this is the focus of your bio as a *BrandFace*. Here are a few other questions to assist in your professional content. Have you published your works before? Received a prestigious award? Served as a board member for a recognizable organization? Are you a member of any trade associations? Have you received press coverage for your accomplishments? Have you co-authored any professional programs? Have you invented a new product?

Your Personal Story:
Keep in mind that your bio might be slightly different for a book. This bio is focused on you as a business owner or leader. There is most likely a compelling reason why you decided to start your business or become a leader in the industry you chose. Tell your story with humor, humility and authenticity. Give it a truly personal touch by sharing things like your hobbies, people who have inspired you, your likes and dislikes, etc.

Media Coverage:
If you have received media coverage, such as an interview with a radio station, mentions in a newspaper article, a guest spot on a local TV news program or even mentions and interviews in a blog or e-zine, list them here. As your *BrandFace* persona evolves, you'll be adding to this section.

PRESS KIT
A press kit is an opportunity to get creative and detailed, and to include other marketing components you've created as a *BrandFace*. Below are several elements I've seen included in press kits. You don't have to utilize all of them, but those that I consider critical are marked with an asterisk. For most purposes, a digital press kit is sufficient, though some professional public

speakers and authors still produce a printed version.

*Pitch Letter:

Your pitch letter (also called a cover or welcome letter) should accompany your press kit. It's your opportunity to tell people why they should view the rest of your press kit, hire you or interview you. Think of it like an elevator pitch. You have mere seconds to communicate the strong points which will motivate someone to push the 'stop' button in order to hear more. A great pitch letter is usually no more than three paragraphs. First, introduce yourself and the reason for your contact. If you are promoting a book, share the publication date and your available dates for appearances. Second, explain why they should be interested in your content, and what their readers, listeners or viewers will learn from you. If there is a topical or even local spin, mention it. Finally, share your contact information and inform them of a specific date you plan to follow up with them.

*Photos:

Include at least three different types of photos for immediate download. These are helpful for the press as well as companies who hire you to speak and might want to include your photo on any materials promoting your appearance. For variety and multi-purpose use, include one head shot, one shot from shoulders up and one shot either sitting on standing. Don't forget to include product photos! If you have images of your book, include those for use on web pages or collateral materials. Provide them in high resolution in case they are being used in print.

*Bio:

Be creative and personal with your biography. If someone is hiring you to speak, it's likely that one of their main objectives is to find someone who will *entertain* as well as inform. If your bio is boring, the assumption is that you are, too. Take a humorous approach or share a personal story as part of your bio.

*Contact Info:

This area of your press kit should include the obvious (phone, email, etc.), but should also include any social media links pertinent to the purpose of your press kit.

*Accomplishments:

Your accomplishments should include all notable events since you founded your business or chose your profession. These can be awards you have received, programs you have created or supported, certifications you have earned, charity efforts you have participated in or any other goals you have accomplished. Presenting these on a timeline is a simple way to tell the story of the evolution of your career.

*Media Coverage:

As mentioned in the bio section, list any place you have received coverage or mentions. If you don't remember the websites or online publications who have mentioned you or your business (or linked to you), there's a simple search trick to find them. Enter "link:http://www.yourdomain.com" into a Google search bar and it should show all mentions and links from other sites (back to your domain). This tip might be able to help you expand the list of coverage that you may have forgotten about.

*Press Releases:

Your press release should focus on the unveiling of your book, speaking series, etc. There are all types of resources online to help you with the formatting of your press release. The main thing to remember is to stay on point and express clearly why this is of importance to the media and public. Tie your subject matter into recent events, mainstream topics or even controversial topics. The more timely your content, the greater the likelihood you'll get some coverage.

Interview Questions:

Compiling a list of questions for an interviewer is one of the best resources you can provide. Think about the questions you most commonly hear from your customers or peers. Questions should address topics such as your background, why you chose your specific topic, how your topic addresses a specific need or challenge, what or who inspired you, past and future projects, etc. It makes the job easier for the interviewers, and ensures that you get intelligent questions (for which, of course, you will already know the answers).

Video:

The most powerful form of online communication, video is your chance to communicate your unique story, speaking style and personality. If you have them, include videos showcasing highlights from your speaking engagements and any press appearances. I highly recommend a specific video about your book or speaking topics which allows people to see why you chose your career path and what they can learn from you. Finally, capture testimonial videos from your clients as well as your event attendees. Grabbing audience response on video right after an event is one way to get phenomenal feedback right after your attendees are all pumped up.

*Speaking Topics:

Most speakers have two or three speaking topics prepared in advance to coordinate with their main focus. You should list the various topics, and make sure to include the fact that you'll customize your existing talks to the audience, as well. Businesses and organizations love to know that you're willing to do some homework to make sure your talk is on point with what the audience is there to learn. Additionally, list your options in terms of the type and length of your talks as well (such as keynotes or half-day seminars).

*Book or Speaking Highlights:

This area should include the takeaway points from your content. What will people learn? Do you feel the content fills a void? How will lives be improved by the content? A short paragraph and some highlighted bullet points should give the overall view of why someone should interview or hire you, and serve as talking points for interviewers.

Sales Copy:

You'll find that people in your network are happy to help you promote your book, talks or products. The hardest part for them is knowing the exact verbiage to use, so help them out! Go ahead and write some copy (in third person) so they can easily copy, paste and send to their network. Consider e-newsletter content, blog posts or social media posts, and provide copy in different lengths for those purposes. You'll find that you get a lot more promotion from your network this way because you don't make them think. They just copy and paste. It's a beautiful thing.

Banner Ads:

One of the best press kits I've seen belongs to Michael Hyatt of Platform Media (MichaelHyatt.com). It's comprehensive, and full of items I didn't even think to include, such as banner ads! There are many businesses, organizations and people in your network who will promote you on their websites, and a professionally designed banner ad which links to your content is perfect and convenient. Design several standard sizes, and provide the links or code for each so they link to the correct page of your site. It's a brilliant idea.

Ron's Message

Tonya's right when she says that people are interested in the story behind the face. They want to know who you are and what you're all about. I teach our team leaders that people buy from people they know, like and trust. Although most people don't really know a lot about how I grew up, the consequences of our childhood have a direct effect on who we are and how we do things. I grew up pretty much on my own. My grandmother raised me till I was seven. I never had traditional parents. My brother and I were in a foster home for seven years, which didn't go too well.

At the age of 14, I struck out on my own and was eventually emancipated at age 16 by the state of Ohio. Those experiences gave me the survival instincts to say, "This too shall pass", no matter what happens. Most people feel that it's horrible, not having parents. But if you didn't have them, you don't know what you're missing. I think it made me mature at a very early age. I just had myself and that was it. As a result, early on, you don't have the sense of direction that a traditional nuclear family brings. I had to find my own direction. I believe that definitely reflects on how I do business today. Instead of excuses, learn it. Anything can be accomplished if you just open your eyes to the possibilities.

Chapter 12:

CRITICAL ELEMENTS OF A
BRANDFACE® WEBSITE

Your main website should be considered your information hub, a prospect's source for everything they need to know about you and your company. It's also the place where your expertise is on full display! Consider it as you would your own magazine, and every *BrandFace* wants their own magazine, right? Here are some tips on making sure your website properly represents your brand and positions you as an authority in your industry.

DOMAIN NAME
When reserving your domain name, I recommend four important guidelines in order to achieve maximum marketing results.

Easy to Recall:
Choose a URL (or domain name) that is easy to remember. For your business website, the company name is usually sufficient as long as it meets the other criteria below.

Easy to Spell:
If your business name is Schlotzwarf's Deli, I'd definitely recommend a different domain name *for marketing purposes*. That doesn't mean you shouldn't own SchlotzwarfsDeli.com. Own it and redirect it to a more marketable domain that is also part of your branding approach. For example, if your tagline is *Your Hometown Deli*, grab YourHometownDeli.com. It's easy to remember and easy to spell. This is especially important if you advertise on radio. But even when you are able to show your domain name on other platforms, don't assume people will immediately visit your site while the URL is in view. They may attempt to do so at a later time, and both recall and ease of spelling become important.

Short and Sweet:
Domain names that are no longer than three words are generally easier to remember. There are some exceptions, of course, such as very specific domain names for search purposes, like GeorgiaHomesForSale.com.

Stick with .com:
I realize it's tempting to reserve a domain name with a .net, .info, .biz or other extension when the *.com* extension you really want is already taken. However,

entering .com into a browser is just a default choice for most visitors, and if someone else already has that domain, your marketing could be inadvertently sending them to a competitor's site—or worse, you may find yourself with a case of trademark infringement. One more thing to consider is content. Don't reserve a domain name with a different extension if the .com owned by someone else contains content you wouldn't want associated with you or your business. For instance, WhiteHouse.gov is the official website of the White House. But *WhiteHouse.com* is a jump page with links to various dating and pornographic sites. I'm sure our recent Presidents have all wondered how their technology experts missed that one!

In addition to your main business website, I recommend that you purchase your own name as a domain name if it is available. For instance, I own TonyaEberhart.com, and redirect that domain to my BrandFaceStar.com website.

MULTI-DEVICE

Before customizing your site for a *BrandFace* approach, it's vital that your visitors be able to view and navigate your website on any device. Otherwise, all that customization goes to waste. Most consumers today view websites on multiple devices (desktop, mobile and tablet), with mobile and tablet online access growing at a very rapid rate. You'll want to make sure your site not only displays well on all screen sizes, but functions well, too. The latest in design is called *responsive* web design, a website which automatically detects the screen size of your device and fluidly adjusts to those parameters. This means web developers no longer need to design multiple sites for multiple devices. This is a plus from both a design and cost perspective! Most popular web design platforms, such as Wordpress, have hundreds of responsive design themes to choose from, and at very reasonable price points. If your current website is not responsive, I strongly suggest you make the switch.

IMAGING

Make sure your face is one of the first things your prospects see when they get to your home page. The familiarity of your friendly face is important, as well as your signature branding images. After all, if people really do buy from a person (and not a logo), you want your friendly mug on there to help close the deal. You can add your photo and branding images in the header of the site, which generally appears on all pages or use it sporadically throughout the pages in different positions, such as graphic images or in widget graphics in the side rails of each page.

INTERACTION

Interacting with your prospects one-to-one on your website is just as important as interacting on social media. In fact, it's generally a more qualified prospect who is reaching out to you through your main site, because it's often the last place they land prior to making email, phone or face-to-face contact. Make it clear how they can ask questions or contact you. I'm a big fan of having your contact information embedded in the header of every page. In addition, set up an area of your site where visitors can ask questions which will be personally answered by you. And if your blog is part of your main site (which I recommend), make sure to respond to comments quickly to keep the dialogue going. You'll learn more about this in the Blog chapter.

GOALS

Your main website should have multiple goals in order to be considered a full scale information hub. The most important goals are listed here, but there certainly could be others. When people visit your site, it says they want to learn more about you and your business. This is usually the homework stage, where they will make a final determination on whether they will take that next step and move from prospect to (one step closer to) becoming a customer.

Inform:

Make sure your site displays all the information your prospects and customers are seeking. If you're not sure about this, it's well worth an informal focus group! Invite friends, peers and acquaintances to peruse your site and give you feedback. Ask them to consider the type of information they would seek as a customer, whether that information was available or easy to find and what they feel your site might be missing. Be sure to include the obvious items such as information about your company, contact information (on all pages, either in the header or footer), hours of operation, product and service offerings, accomplishments and more. One of my clients lists all media on which he has been featured, which adds instant credibility.

Educate:

Start with letting your prospects know how you're different. Remember, "It's better to be different than it is to be better." (*22 Immutable Laws of Marketing*, Al Reis & Jack Trout). Getting people to your website is somewhat equivalent to the old consumer path of getting them on the phone or to your door. They're obviously interested in learning more, and it's your opportunity to tell them why they should do business with you versus your competitors. You can do this through various means, like tips and advice, educational product or service videos, downloadable e-books, etc.

Contact Capture:

Lead generation is certainly a goal of most websites. You want to capture a list of people willing to receive information from you on a regular basis. Most of the time, this contact info is utilized for email marketing purposes or mobile marketing, such as text messaging. There are several ways to get prospects to hand over this information, and almost all of those include either giving them important information or a special offer. The Email Marketing chapter discusses this in detail.

Conversion:
The ultimate goal is achieved when a prospect turns into a customer. Conversion can occur on several levels according to your goals at the time, such as sign-ups for your newsletter, video views, downloads, etc., but generally the end goal is when the visitor converts from prospect to paying customer.

CONTENT
Carefully consider the content for your site and put the most important items right at the fingertips of your prospects. There's an excellent book on web design that I often recommend. It's called *Don't Make Me Think: A Common Sense Approach to Web Usability,* by Steve Krug. I love the name, in terms of both the book and marketing via the web. When your website is aesthetically pleasing, informative, entertaining and organized for ease of use, that perception of professionalism extends to you as a *BrandFace.* Here are some content items for consideration when determining what's most important to your prospects and customers.

About:
Keep this section brief but interesting. People are attracted to a great story, something I like to call the human element. For instance, I'm from a small town in North Georgia called Dawsonville. It's known for generations of moonshiners and being the catalyst for the auto racing industry. Those facts alone open the conversation in an interesting way, and allow me to share some of the highlights of my background. I consider myself very fortunate to have grown up in that small town, and attribute that environment to many of my accomplishments today. Our unique stories are what makes us human, and it's that connection that people appreciate and identify with beyond just business. Don't be afraid to share your story, especially to the degree with which it shaped your professional aspirations and led you to your position today as a *BrandFace.*

Contact:
Again, make sure the basic contact information such as your email, phone and address are prominent on every page of the site. The best option is to embed the information into your header or footer. In addition, include a separate contact page, which displays your photo, a brief bio (unless you display that

on a separate 'author' or 'about' page). Add your social media links so visitors can become fans and followers. You can also post photos and bios of your team members as well. This does not detract from your *BrandFace* status. In fact, it enhances it, as it shows your dedication to the team that has helped to build your successful business.

Video:
There's an entire chapter on Video Marketing, and rightfully so! As a *BrandFace*, you'll want the most personal marketing tool to be front and center as soon as your visitors reach your site. On the home page, I usually recommend an 'about' video, featuring your own personal and professional story. At times, however, it's great to switch out that video in order to promote a new product, service, event, promotion or initiative, especially if it's something that you're advertising on other platforms. Make sure the video player is large enough for viewing without the need to expand to full screen, or that you use a widget which opens the video in a larger pop-up window. I've been asked my opinion on video that automatically plays when visitors first get to your site. Frankly, it's one of my biggest pet peeves. Don't do this! Allow your visitors to make the decision themselves. They're smart enough to push the play button. Don't force them to curse and search for the volume or stop button.

Blog:
You'll read much more about this in the Blog chapter, but I do recommend having your blog as part of your main site, on the same domain. Though it's easy enough to just link out to your standalone blog from your main site, having it built within your site can help tremendously with search optimization for your information hub, your main website.

Products & Services:
If you have a lot of products and services, you might consider a category page with icons or thumbnails that jump to individual pages. This helps to make your site more organized and user-friendly, rather than having so much content on one page that your visitors must endlessly scroll. I call these 'toilet paper' pages. On each product or service page, I recommend utilizing video and/or photos as well as a brief description. Avoid the urge to use too much text. I realize that text is important to search engines, but I'm a firm believer that you can mix a beautifully organized design with good information and enough relevant keywords to get the job done.

Sign Up:
This option can vary (Join, Subscribe, etc.) but it's generally used for visitors to sign up to receive your e-newsletter, e-magazine, etc. This is a main

objective of your site so you'll want to make sure this option is either on all pages (in the sidebar, for instance) or that the option is part of your top navigation choices. I prefer both places. Think of it like asking for the sale! Attempt to close every chance you get.

Testimonials:
The only thing more powerful than sharing your point of differentiation is when your customers share it for you! Ask customers to talk about their experience with you. Document it on video whenever possible, even if it's a rudimentary video versus professionally produced. And figure out a way to leverage those testimonials onto other platforms. Ask your customer's permission to repeat those on social media outlets, your company collateral materials and even in your advertising.

Market/Shop:
This is the area of your site which features your ecommerce options. A lot of speakers and authors will need this option. Put all your marketable items here, even if they are free! Mix your free items in with paid items in order to build and show the value of your content. Enter a price beside each item, and strike through the price on those items you wish to provide for free. This will instantly give visitors the perception of lots of valuable material! Jeffrey Gitomer is known as one of the country's most accomplished experts in sales training and speaking. His website, Gitomer.com, provides an excellent example of ecommerce and a preview of his expertise materials. There are plenty of easy, affordable plug-ins available for ecommerce for Wordpress and other web design platforms.

Speaking:
You're a *BrandFace*, so of course you'll speak publicly from time to time! Even if it's not a revenue generator for you, you should still prepare at least one talk and post any speaking topics on your site. If you infrequently speak, this area can fall under 'services' in your main navigation. If, on the other hand, you are asked to speak often, consider adding 'speaking' as a main navigation link. Include bullet points about the topics you cover as well as any takeaways your audience can expect. Add testimonials to this page, too, but make them specific to your speaking talents.

Press:
Make it easy for media outlets to provide coverage of you and your company by including a press area on your main site. This is where you'll share any press releases and your press kit, full of tons of information designed to get you hired, promoted or published! There's an entire area describing your press kit in the Public Relations chapter. Even if this area is seldom used by

members of the press, it's very impressive to visitors and definitely implies importance, authority and credibility.

Book:
If you have written a book, e-book, white paper, etc., make sure that information is in your main navigation and promoted prominently on your home page. It's your star material. You'll want to share some highlights from the publication so visitors get an idea of the content. If it's a full size book, include a sneak peek inside (the first few chapters) as well. And of course, a link to order the book.

Calendar:
If you do lots of speaking engagements and appearances, you might consider a calendar of events for your main site. There are some impressive apps that will also incorporate booking functionality through the calendar, which will allow visitors to instantly book you through the site according to your open dates.

Thank You:
This is a truly important and often over-looked step. When someone takes a step toward conversion, such as purchasing your book or filling out a form to request speaking services, you should always direct them to a personalized 'thank you' page. The ultimate option for this page is a thank you video which expresses your gratitude for purchasing the book, etc. The second best option is a page with your photo, a personal thank you message from you and your actual signature. It's a relatively small thing, but it goes a long way toward building your reputation and image as a *BrandFace*.

-------------------- **Ron's Message** --------------------

Your website is often the very first impression people get of you and your business. It's critical to our business. We have one of the highest performing websites in the industry because we work every day to make sure it has the most current and credible tips and advice for our customers. As a result, our conversion rate (visitors to customers) is outstanding.

Among all that educational material, though, I feel it's important to express the human element. When people get to our website, it should portray exactly the persona and brand they see in our videos and all our other marketing. That kind of consistency is critical. A large percentage of our customers visit our site before they reach out to us to book an appointment, so we want to make sure that the trust and credibility they sense in our advertising messages is continued there. And by our high conversion rate, we know that trust factor is there.

Example C: The Basement Doctor website

Chapter 13:

THE BOUNTIFUL BENEFITS
OF BLOGGING

According to Urban Dictionary, a blog is defined as "a meandering, blatantly uninteresting online diary that gives the author the illusion that people are interested in their stupid, pathetic life". Though a humorous approach, I can't always argue against that definition. I've visited many blogs that are as self-serving and pompous as one of the housewives on reality TV. However, like anything in life, there is good and bad.

The truth is, a blog can be one of the most effective marketing tools available today, especially if you are the face of your brand. If you've hesitated to blog because you feel it's only for egomaniacs, here are a few reasons you should reconsider—and how to execute it with humility:

BENEFITS OF A BLOG
Expertise:
A blog is one of the best ways to establish expertise. When properly positioned, your blog can set the tone for how people view you and your company. If you focus your content on helping others through your specific industry knowledge, it can set you apart from the crowd—and the focus becomes your expertise instead of your ego. A good rule of thumb is to keep at least 75% of your posts positive—an occasional rant is entertaining, but too much negativity can make you appear unapproachable.

Cost-Efficient:
A blog costs little to nothing to operate. The internet is a great equalizer in this way. There are many great blog platforms and templates to choose from which can highlight you and your industry well. A few of the more popular blog platforms are Blogger, Wordpress and Tumblr.

Credibility:
A blog can help you build credibility, especially if you keep your ego in check. If visitors see post after post of great information and advice, that consistency builds trust. But combine that with seeing your face, and hearing your voice and name throughout all your marketing efforts, and it creates familiarity, even if they haven't yet met you. Just remember to treat your blog readers with respect. Respond to their comments with sincerity and humility, even when they disagree. People notice how you treat others, and it can have a big

impact on how they view you—both professionally and personally.

Social Connections:
A blog can serve as the hub for your social efforts. In other words, many roads can lead back to your blog--Facebook, Twitter, LinkedIn, Pinterest, etc. By teasing your latest blog post on social media, you can drive your fans and followers straight to the relevant content they seek. The consistency of knowledge across all platforms emphasizes your expertise, leaving ego questions in the dust.

Engagement:
A blog is the perfect platform for your readers to comment and engage with you. I recommend setting your comments area to require your approval before posting, but you should approve and respond quickly to the legitimate posts. Monitoring and responding to comments gives you an excellent idea of the topics that spark the most discussion and debate, and will give you an indication of the direction of your content moving forward.

PLATFORM RECOMMENDATION
There are many resources that can help you set up a blog or determine which platform to use. I've used Tumblr and Wordpress. My personal recommendation is to use Wordpress for your entire site and make your blog one page within the overall site. This approach provides the following benefits:

Convenience:
It means only one login when it's time to update your site. If you have an ever-growing spreadsheet of passwords like mine, I know you'll appreciate this one.

Template Choices:
Wordpress is an open source platform, meaning there are thousands of developers who have customized attractive and functional templates and plug-ins to highlight you and your business. Before I chose the Wordpress template for my *BrandFace* site, I made a list of the attributes I desired, and then began my search. In addition, there are companies who will take a custom design and convert it to a Wordpress theme.

Content Management System:
I've worked with several content management systems, and Wordpress combines ease of use with limitless possibilities. Though every template has restrictions, if you do your homework in advance, you should be able to execute anything you need on your site.

Tutorials:
Wordpress.org is a thorough resource. While there is no Wordpress support staff, there is an enormous network of Wordpress experts out there to answer any question.

Customization:
As a *BrandFace*, your photo should be prominent on your blog. Using your image across all platforms is the key to consistent marketing practices. The best way to accomplish this is to include your image in the header so it appears on all pages. There are hundreds of Wordpress themes which will allow you to customize the header, side rails and page content.

BLOG CONTENT

Finally, wondering how you'll come up with blog topics that emphasize your expertise and not your ego? To start, blog content should focus entirely on helping others through your knowledge and expertise. In addition to the content topic suggestions in the Content Marketing chapter, here are a few more slightly different twists which are customized for blog content.

Product/Service Reviews:
Look at the top selling products for your industry or company, and give honest feedback about each (tackle each product in a separate blog post). A good 'pros and cons' post is helpful, as it helps your readers weigh their options.

Topical News:
Pay attention to recent news and give advice or tips on popular topics. For instance, if you own a roofing company and a wind storm has just hit your community, discuss best practices and guidelines for choosing the right contractor for the job.

Misconceptions:
List the top misconceptions in your industry and tell your readers why those are incorrect. This helps to position you and your company as truthful problem-solvers and also tackles any customer objections in advance.

Interviews:
Interview someone interesting who serves as a good example in your industry. People who work in businesses that complement yours, a client who has had positive results, or even a competitor. Interviewing competitors is a tactic which can truly position you as an authority. This works especially well if you are also selling products or services to these competitors. Write about their

insights, explore how and why they do what they do, and how your readers can learn from them.

Reviews:
Read an industry-related book or share a video and write an honest review. If you disagree with the content, say so. If you love it, the author just might be your next interview.

Events:
Each time you attend an event, blog about it. Tell your readers why you attended, and share things you learned that would be of importance to them. Link out to the event website and in turn, they may link back.

Case Studies:
Share a good customer case study in an interesting way. Yes, facts and numbers are great, but nothing is better than a good story. Ask your customer's permission to include their name and photo in your blog post. Leverage this into a testimonial for you or your business.

Daily Life:
Share things in your daily life that might be important to your readers. If you buy a new car or tackle a home improvement project, share how your experience might relate to your industry or customers.

Features:
Each week, choose one day to write on the same topic. It could be 'Customer Service Monday', where you share the customer service experiences you had the previous week. Encourage your readers to share as well. Doing this will ensure that you have at least one regular blog post weekly.

BLOGGING TIPS
Blogging Frequency:
One of my clients says he only blogs when he has something important to say. I love the fact that he only wants to turn out meaningful content, but bloggers need to strike a delicate balance between the importance and frequency of content. My general rule of thumb is that a blog should be updated at least once a week. And if you don't feel as though you have something important to say, work harder at it. Refresh your memory bank by referring back to some of the blog topic categories in this chapter to spark creativity. Almost everything around you is a potential blog article if you think creatively and connect it to what your own prospects and customers are experiencing or may need to know.

Length of Posts:
As a general rule, most blog posts average between 500 and 1000 words, but the most important aspect is the content itself. A blog post should inform, educate or entertain. When informing or educating, ask yourself whether you could have been more concise in your blog. Could you have gotten your point across in fewer words? If so, it's likely that your post is too long. On the flip side, you can bet it's too short if you find that you haven't accurately answered the questions your post was intended to answer.

Auto-Posts:
Take advantage of the ability to enter your posts now, but have them publish at a later date. You should see this option near your publish button. This is an excellent time saver. If you're like me, you'll occasionally get on a writing kick and generate several posts at once.

Exclusive Content:
A lot of bloggers will re-post the work of others, and some do so simply to fulfill a blogging quantity goal. I do believe that re-posting other blogs a great idea, and of course commenting on their work with your own opinions and spin is an excellent *BrandFace* strategy. However, the most impactful content is your own. Consider a guideline of at least 60% of your own exclusive content when blogging.

Comments:
On or off? It's a question asked by many beginning bloggers. And the answer is...turn them on, but in your admin area set them to require pre-approval before posting. That way, you retain the ability to interact with your visitors (that's the purpose of a blog!) and screen possible inappropriate comments.

Promotion:
One of your marketing goals should be to entice your visitors to subscribe to your blog. That means that each time you post, the link will come to them via their blog feed, inbox or mobile app. There are some simple apps which update each time you post a new blog.

Themes:
One of the blogging strategies I've implemented in the past is posting according to a theme. For instance, each Friday I shared a personal experience, such as a customer service story or my encounter with another *BrandFace*. Think about doing 'Motivational Mondays', 'Free Download Fridays' or (if you're a pet lover), post a photo of an adoptable pet each week.

It's the personal, human element that makes us relatable, so don't be afraid to weave your personal or philanthropic initiatives into the mix.

Ron's Message

I don't do a lot of the blogging myself, but I do certainly recognize the importance of it. Search engine optimization is critical to the success of any website and business today. We share all kinds of information on our blog. One of the most effective things we've done on our blog is post video (which we'll discuss more later).

We blog about educational topics regularly, because you never know when someone is seeking a solution to their basement problem, and we want to be sure the resources we provide are thorough. We also blog about our charity affiliations quite often. It magnifies our involvement and good works throughout our community. And like us, or even more so, charitable organizations and associations need the additional mentions and awareness, too.

Chapter 14:

ESTABLISH EXPERTISE THROUGH CONTENT MARKETING

Though content marketing falls into many other categories within this book, it deserves its own chapter. First, let's define it. Content marketing is "the creation or contribution of exclusive and valuable content or information designed to share with your potential or current customers for the purpose of establishing expertise in your field and building trust and relationships over time".

Regularly sharing your knowledge about a particular industry, category or subject can elevate you to expert status and help you master being the face of your brand. Without great content, it's virtually impossible to elevate yourself as an expert. From e-publications and videos to blog articles and more, content marketing is perhaps the most important element of marketing in terms of search. When a potential customer begins to search for a company to provide a solution, they most often begin that search online. Rather than rely on an advertising message, they seem more concerned with trusted opinions and expertise. In addition, relevant content greatly reduces (and often eliminates) the need to spend large amounts of money on search engine optimization or search marketing.

Great content should be further defined as truthful, relevant, purposeful and transparent. Let's look at each of these attributes:

Truthful:
As one of my clients once said to me, "If you lie about your business, it *will* catch up with you. You don't have a choice about being truthful today. The truth is online, out there for everyone to see." With the ability to post reviews virtually anywhere, including review sites such as the Better Business Bureau, Angie's List and Yelp, you really can't escape the opinions of your customers. Notice I didn't say *truth*, but opinions. As every business owner knows, customers are as fickle as feathers in the wind. One honest mistake can leave you scrambling to regain public trust. That's why the existence of truthful content in advance of any potential negative reviews is essential in setting the stage for expertise and gaining the confidence of your customer base.

Relevant:

Email marketing research studies in recent years have shown that non-relevant content is among the top three reasons people opt out of content subscriptions. When someone gives you permission to send them information and advice, take it seriously. Do what you say you will do—send them exactly the content they agreed to receive. Think in terms of the *quality* of your customers versus quantity. Every business is seeking serious customers, those who will not only become repeat customers, but will spread the positive word about you to their network of family and friends. And serious customers follow you, friend you, subscribe and recommend you for specific reasons.

Purposeful:

Each time you create or contribute content, think about the reasons people are following you, and the problems you are trying to solve. Are you recommending a new app that makes life more convenient for the busy traveler? Are you providing a checklist for someone who is about to hire a remodeling company? Are you sharing home remedy options for pets that have allergies? Whatever your advice, consider what your core customer is seeking in terms of response, and be specific. Give them answers they won't find anywhere else! Every day, millions of bits of content are created online, and I think we'd all agree that most of it is just plain boring, created to meet the quantity quota instead of the quality quota. Think about how you would appreciate a thorough and thoughtful answer. Furthermore, don't be afraid to share your best advice. Once that advice is published by you, you become the authority. The beautiful thing about the internet is that everything is time stamped, so if your competitor steals your information and attempts to pass it off as their own, the next rule comes into play...*transparency.*

Transparent:

I continue to have conversations and debates with business owners about this issue. How much information should you share? Is there such a thing as being too open, too vulnerable? My argument is that transparency already exists among your customers each time they share an opinion online, about you or your competitors. Yes, there are some things that you should not disclose as part of a common sense business strategy; for instance, prematurely sharing information about new products or services. This could give your competitors a heads up on your business or marketing strategy. When it comes to posting rates and fees, I believe this should be handled on a case by case basis.

By now I'm sure you're excited to create some content! Let's start with suggestions for finding the most comfortable way for you to get the information out of your head, and then we'll tackle content topic suggestions and various forms of content.

GET IT OUT

So how do you extract all that great content your brain has been holding onto all these years? The answer is, in whatever manner is most comfortable and convenient to you. Here are some suggestions to consider.

Video:

Some people are very comfortable in front of a camera, so we set the camera rolling as we ask questions and simply capture the answers with no script. If I had to choose, this is the preferable format for extracting content. Video is such a valuable part of marketing today, and if you start here, the rest is easy. I've found the most popular type in terms of building credibility is called the *BrandFace* interview style video, when the client is not looking directly into the camera, but appearing to look at the interviewer just off-camera. These types of videos are similar to those you may see on shows such as *60 Minutes* or *20/20*. If you are shooting the video yourself, without any assistance, you can even stage this by focusing on something just to the left or right of the camera as you attempt to answer questions you think your prospects would ask. An additional tip: shoot with a green screen behind you so you can insert any kind of background you'd like for marketing purposes.

Audio:

I have conducted simple audio recording sessions with several clients in order to get their answers to content questions. I find that it's extremely helpful because neither of us has to take notes during the session, allowing us both to stay focused on a productive back-and-forth dialogue. When the session is complete, those answers are transcribed so we can use them in practically any content form. A helpful tip: when you change subjects or topics during your recording session, stop and start the recorder so it's easier for the person who will transcribe the audio to separate the content by subject matter. You can use practically any recording device or software for this purpose. There are some great phone, tablet and computer apps for that purpose. I use a digital audio recorder for two reasons. First, it's small and portable, so I can take it anywhere. Second, the digital quality is superb, so if I'd like to use the recorded audio for podcasts or even in conjunction with a video, it's ready. I also carry a lapel microphone that plugs directly into the recorder. If I clip it to the subject's shirt or jacket, the microphone stays at a consistent distance from their voice and ensures good sound quality. I have not personally used *Dragon Speaking* software (which translates audio to text), but I understand that it can be a very effective tool for those who prefer to speak their thoughts and have them auto-transcribed. It's a great time-saver if you prefer audio over video or writing.

Writing:
If you prefer writing to capture your thoughts, there are some great note-taking apps to keep your thoughts organized by category or subject matter. I use Evernote on both my laptop and smartphone to record thoughts in separate notebooks or categories. It syncs between my computer and phone nicely, so no matter where the notes originated, I can view them both places. If you use a mixture of ways to record your content like I do, you'll love Evernote's voice recording capabilities as well. It gives you the best of both worlds in a reliable platform. However, there are many other apps that will serve the purpose of convenience and reliability for recording content.

CONTENT TOPICS
Here are some topic suggestions for creating content that is truthful, relevant, purposeful and transparent. You are limited only by your imagination, creativity and experiences!

Frequently Asked Questions:
Write down the top questions you consistently hear from clients or prospects. This is a great indication of curiosity in your industry, and you can be the expert that provides the answers. Based on your conversations over the years, you already know most of these questions. If you're stumped, ask your customers or other business leaders to help you by submitting a few questions they have about your industry.

Tips & Advice:
Do you ever wish you had shortcuts to success? So do your customers! And this is your chance to allow them to learn from you so they can avoid some of the same pitfalls that you have already experienced. This kind of information is priceless coming from an authority who has 'been there, done that'. For instance, I learned one of the most valuable lessons about negotiating and pricing consulting contracts from a mentor who, unfortunately, had to learn from his own mistakes. I was lucky enough to reap the rewards of his misfortune. Your customers will thank you for it. You'll find your greatest return on investment regarding content from this category.

Experiences:
Your unique experiences as a business owner and leader are valuable to others. We live in a voyeuristic society, as evidenced by the multitude of reality shows. There will always be some people who are interested in your favorite meal, where you shop for groceries, with whom you dine, where you vacation, other businesses you'd recommend, etc. Sharing a few of these

experiences, especially as they may relate to your profession, can help you bond with your fans and followers.

Numbered Lists:
An example would be 'Top 8 Uses for Web Video'. Numbered lists are great to capture attention, and very popular because they are usually a quick read. It implies that you've done your homework by producing a list of focused tips on a subject. If you're looking for ideas, start with your Frequently Asked Questions document and see if it makes sense to do a numbered list with some of those answers. Practically any business related question has a finite number of answers, and you can usually list them in priority order, which is just one reason numbered lists are so popular.

Get Started:
Consider content that helps someone learn the first steps associated with a particular project or goal, such as 'Quick Start Guide to Shooting Video'. When you share information like this, think about how you can leverage business from this. An example is a hardscapes company that specializes in paver patios. Each year in the spring, they host free clinics at their retail location which teach homeowners how to install their own patio. Even though they employ installers and do a respectable amount of installation business, they realize that there is an entire category of Do It Yourselfers that could still become customers. When the clinic is complete, the attendees not only leave with a complete how-to guide, they can choose and purchase their materials on the spot at the retail location. This business even offers rental equipment to complete the job. This allows them to capture an entire audience segment who might otherwise end up at Lowe's or Home Depot.

Did You Know:
Share historical facts such as 'this day in history', unusual things and especially information that will give your fans and followers the edge. Statistics about your industry, breaking news and local stories of relevance are just a few that belong in this category.

Customer Service:
With so many businesses on social media these days, it's often faster to get a customer service response on a social platform rather than by phone or email. This creates an excellent opportunity not only to showcase great things your customers say about you, but to resolve issues out in the open so the Twitter-verse can see how you handle conflict. Whether you like it or not, your business practices are on display for the world to see. The conversation is taking place with or without you. Wouldn't you rather be involved?

FORMS OF CONTENT

Each of the following forms of content is explored in further detail in other chapters throughout the book, but here's a snippet for each to get you started.

Blog:

A blog is the quintessential expertise vehicle! One of my favorites is OrganizedDreams.com, a blog we helped to create with Stephanie Antunez, a multiple franchise owner with California Closets. Their specialty is organization that is also beautiful. They provide storage solutions for every area of the home, from a closet to the garage. Stephanie is relatively new as the face of her brand, and relates to her customers very well, which is just one of the reasons she does an excellent job as a *BrandFace*. On her blog, she shares organizational tips and advice, along with a section called *Stephanie's Favorite Things* (a compilation of 'Food, Fun, Fashion and Furnishings'). Each month, she chooses a feature photograph in each category to represent her favorite, and links out to those photos on Pinterest. This strategy gives her followers a glimpse into her own personal style.

E-Books:

An e-book is simply an electronic book that can be read on a computer or handheld electronic device. E-books can be any length, but the most popular are between 10-15 pages and provide information about a specific topic. They generally have graphics or images to support the content, as well.

White Papers:

A white paper is a document or guide that is laser focused on explaining an issue, solving a problem, highlighting products or services or providing instruction on a specific topic. Unlike e-books, white papers are usually more technical in nature, almost like an instruction manual. They range in length, but are most common between 8-10 pages. The best white papers include an interesting story or two to support the stats or instruction.

Videos:

The most versatile form of content, videos are powerful marketing tools. When you can't be in front of a prospect one-to-one, they're the next best thing to being there. Much more detailed information is available in the *Video* chapter.

Podcasts:

Technically, podcasts can be audio or video, but most people still refer to podcasts as their original audio form. Don't underestimate the power of the spoken word. I personally listen to audio books and podcasts while exercising, and I imagine there are millions more like me. If you produce content than can be separated into smaller pieces, it allows you to upload your podcasts in different formats (short form and long form) so your listeners/viewers can ingest at their own speed or in unison with other activities. There are many platforms for downloading and subscribing to podcasts, but the most popular is iTunes.

Books:
With today's self-publishing options, anyone can become an author! Traditional books are great, but think beyond the ordinary and look at some unique options like mini-books. These are smaller than standard books (about half the size) and make great promotional tools. Start with a single step and outline what your book would include. That will serve as your guide for progress. If you break the content into bite-size pieces, you'll find the process is much easier than you imagined. I have found it's easiest to separate my chapters into separate documents during the writing process (rather than one long-running document). That allows me to either change the name of each chapter as it's completed, or pull them into a separate file. It's also much easier to write and edit in chapters because you don't have to scroll through an enormous document as you work.

Infographics:
An information graphic is a visual image in a graphic format which helps us to understand a process, system or other information more easily. They are very popular on social media platforms like Facebook and Pinterest (which is known for images).

Magazines:
Magazines are an aesthetically pleasing way to present your content and can be created in various styles. Consider a company mini-magazine featuring your background, mission statement, products and services. A traditional magazine approach could promote an entire category, with all content provided by your business. If you own a landscape nursery, you can launch an outdoor living magazine. If you own a restaurant, you can launch a local cuisine magazine. One of the most interesting new platforms I've witnessed is called *Flipboard*, which gives you the ability to build your own online magazine. The possibilities are limitless. Magazines can become revenue producers for your company as well if you sell ads to other businesses seeking the same audience as you.

Slide Presentations:
Think of all the presentations your company may have and put those to work for you! *Slideshare* is a professional content sharing platform which allows its users to upload slide presentations including infographics, video, audio,

documents and webinars. *Slideshare* presentations can be embedded on websites and blogs, and easily shared across social platforms. It's a social platform, itself, allowing its users to comment, 'like' and build profile pages. In 2012, LinkedIn purchased *Slideshare*, making it a powerful combination of professional networking and content-sharing.

Talks:
Don't let this one frighten you! Speaking in front of a live audience is one of the most effective ways to get your company message across as the face of the brand. Most of the anxiety that comes with public speaking is due to being unprepared. See more details and suggestions in the chapter on Public Speaking.

Seminars & Webinars:
This approach can go hand in hand with your slide presentations on a matter of expertise. If you are a financial institution, you can host webinars on preparing for retirement, choosing the right health insurance or funding for college educations. Keep prospects on the hook longer by presenting a seminar or webinar series which takes place over several weeks. Then remember to upload them to *Slideshare* and other platforms!

BONUS EXAMPLES
There are so many content marketing examples in this book in other areas, but I've added a few additional ones here just to keep the creativity flowing!

Using Bloggers:
Good Greens bars were developed by Keith Pabley in 2011 to fill the void for recently banned junk foods in his area and to provide a healthy and tasty option to all the bad-tasting ones on the market. Keith worked with a physician to ensure that the bars are gluten-free, dairy-free, vegan and contain the nutritional equivalent of 100 percent of the recommended daily amount of fruits and vegetables. He didn't have a large advertising budget, so he built relationships with bloggers to review his product and share opinions. Now Good Greens bars are sold in over 1200 stores.

Humorous Video:
Comedian Michael Dubin and entrepreneur Mark Levine founded *Dollar Shave Club* in 2011 to compete with expensive, brand-name razors. They offer high quality razors for just a dollar a month, sent right to the customer's door. The YouTube video that launched their campaign and ecommerce site helped them attract thousands of customers in just two days. They now have approximately 20 team members in their California office and have attracted millions from investors.

Short Form Video:
Lowe's cleverly uses Vine (six second videos) to demonstrate simple home improvement solutions on Tumblr. They call the series 'Fix in Six". It's a brilliant way to show consumers quick and easy fixes to common, everyday problems.

Educational Video:
An official *BrandFace* client, Michael owns a real estate company in North Georgia. Faced with prospective home buyers who were hesitant to sign an exclusive Buyers Agency Agreement, Michael delivered a brilliant presentation on how doing so would benefit and protect the buyer, and allow his agents to become their 'best friend' throughout the sometimes complex process of purchasing a home.

—————————— **Ron's Message** ——————————

You have to share your knowledge if you want to become the expert. No one has put in more work or accomplished more in the industry, and we need to be certain that we display that in our content on a regular basis. Our website, collateral materials and videos are a testament to this concept and also share a common look and feel to support the brand.

At the end of the day, the goal is to be remembered as the expert, the authority. I feel the best way to do that is to be real and honest about the problem and what it takes to fix it right the first time. We are not the cheapest in the market, at least not by regular standards of service price comparisons. But we *are* the least expensive when it comes to getting the job done right the first time. I run into past customers on almost a daily basis who tell me that we fixed a leak in their basement 15 years ago and it's still dry. They take pride in that and so do I. It's a good feeling.

I'm fortunate to have a staff that assists with all our content generation. As the head of a business, you can't do it all yourself, and it's OK to admit that. If you are responsible for contributing your own content, just remember that if you create it once, you can use it in multiple places. Every piece of our content is published on our blog, our social platforms, some of our collateral materials and even in our email newsletters.

Example D: Bowed or Cracked Walls video

Chapter 15:

COMMANDING AUTHORITY
THROUGH PUBLIC SPEAKING

As mentioned in the chapter on content, don't be afraid of speaking in front of an audience! If you only prepare one talk, make it meaningful and memorable…and most importantly, make certain it states your point of differentiation! People are enthralled with a good story, and most *BrandFace* candidates have a unique story to share. Once you craft your story, you'll need to determine your ideal booking opportunities. Then you'll decide on a sales and promotional strategy. Finally, follow-up is critical to the growth of your customer base. Here are some tips and suggestions for all of these steps.

SPEAKING OPPORTUNITIES
There are many opportunities to speak in front of an audience. Once you become aware of these, the toughest decision is which ones will be most impactful for you and your business. Decide in advance whether you'd like to get paid for every appearance. Some business leaders can command a high price and make it happen, and others are happy to simply get their message out to as many people as possible, whatever the platform. When I first started speaking, my biggest challenge was deciding what I would charge for my talks, and whether I'd consider doing some of them for free. Here are some guidelines which may help you determine which opportunities are right for you.

Paid Opportunities:
For those situations when I am asked to speak in front of an audience that really isn't my target audience (in other words, there is little likelihood that I could sell them a book, training session, marketing audit or consulting program), I will request the full amount for my speaking session. Selling products or services as part of a speaking arrangement is often called 'back of the room' sales. You need to have this discussion with the company that is hiring you first to determine their expectations or policies for selling products and services at the event. While some companies do not allow it, ones that do allow it prefer that you do not spend your speaking time selling yourself. My own personal stance on this is that you should never blatantly sell yourself or your products or services during your talk. If you do a great job with the content your audience is seeking, you won't have to. Your expertise will draw

people to you once the talk is completed.

Sales & Promotional Opportunities:
If I have a specific product to service or sell, I don't mind booking speaking sessions for a reduced fee, as long as the audience members are my target prospects and there is a high likelihood that I can generate revenue from back of the room sales. I get these lower paying requests most often from organizations, associations and charities which may have limited funding to hire speakers. I also look at the number of people in the audience, and weigh that against the time it takes me to prepare for the talk and travel to the speaking location. All of those things come into play when making the decision to accept the lower paying opportunities.

Creating Your Own Event:
Businesses often create their own events in order to attract exactly the kind of prospects they are seeking. For instance, a bank president hosts a quarterly financial seminar on issues like investment, retirement and health care. By creating their own agenda and promoting their own event, they have greater control over who attends, which means more qualified candidates. I'm a big fan of these types of events because they afford you a chance to set your own platform and purpose as a *BrandFace*.

Leverage Opportunities:
On occasion, I have accepted speaking engagements for the sole purpose of leveraging other opportunities. For instance, I have agreed to do lower paying or free talks in order to have an audience with very influential prospects. This is a strategic business move, and it's quite common. If I've had difficulty getting face time with a prospect that I'd like to add to my client roster, and I know they will be in attendance at a particular event, it might be worth the time I invest in booking that event.

Pro Bono Opportunities:
As a *BrandFace*, one of the toughest things to do is say no. After all, you're promoting a friendly, helpful persona who gives back to the community, and the last thing you want to do is disappoint or anger your public. So when you get those heart-tugging requests from local charities and other worthwhile organizations, what should you do? Accept some of them, of course. But also realize that you can't speak for all of them. If you develop and share a clear plan of action regarding pro bono speaking, this helps tremendously with your ability to remain above the fray while still exhibiting compassion for their cause. Personally, I set aside six talks per year for charity organizations. Once those slots are full, they're full, and they're available on a first come-first served basis. This strategy allows me to give back, but also to limit my time

reasonably so I can run my business profitably. Since instituting this plan, each person I have shared it with has been very understanding. I know other business leaders who decide that they will support a specific number of charities each year, and they decide on those in advance. For instance, one auto dealer supports two causes: childhood obesity and the dangers of texting while driving. So everything they do with non-profits centers around those two initiatives.

Negotiations:

As entrepreneurs, we can get very creative when negotiating business deals. Apply this creativity to your speaking sessions as well. In the past, I have agreed to speak for a charity in order to get a long term consulting deal with a prospect. I have developed bundled product/service packages that combine selling the products of the business I'm speaking for along with my own products in order to provide the audience a win-win combination. There will be a few co-branded versions of this book, as well, which will give me opportunities to bring along some of my super star clients to future speaking sessions so audiences can get a double dose of *BrandFace* expertise! Think about ways you can assist each other, and if you approach each opportunity with a spirit of partnership, everyone wins.

GETTING PREPARED
Craft Your Story:

This one shouldn't be too difficult. You're there to talk about *you* and at least some facet of your business, and who knows that better than, well, you? First, think about the most compelling part of your story. Were you told you couldn't or shouldn't start your business? Were you discouraged to claim the marketing position you now occupy? Is your profession of choice an unusual one for someone like you? Was there some specific incident that took place which led you down this business path? Was there someone along the way who inspired you to become the business leader you are today? People attend speaking engagements to learn practical things about business, but if you asked them what was most memorable about the event, they usually repeat the personal stories. The human element is a strong phenomenon.

Know Your Audience:

Think about what the audience hopes to gain from the experience. Are they there to be motivated? Are they there to learn about a specific product or service? Are they there because they have something in common with you? Put yourself in their shoes and do your best to deliver a talk that is customized to their purpose for attending. There is truly no faster way to connect than speaking someone else's language. Take the time to do your homework in advance, even if this means personally contacting a few attendees to interview them about their specific needs with regard to the event.

Advanced Greetings:

It's better to speak to a roomful of friends and acquaintances rather than strangers. So arrive at your event early and introduce yourself personally to the guests as they enter the room. Prior to the event, you may have access to see the roster of people who will be attending. If so, this provides an excellent opportunity to connect prior to the event. Follow those attendees on Twitter and send a select few (your best prospects, of course) a direct message such as, "I see you've signed up to attend the event on Friday (name the event). I'm looking forward to meeting you in person. If there's anything specific you'd like to learn during the event, please don't hesitate to share and I'll do my best to work it in." You'd be amazed how special this can make people feel, and how kindly they will speak of you due to that one simple gesture.

Your Introduction:

Don't expect your emcee or host to write your introduction. It's common to provide that in advance. Even if you write it yourself (which many do), have someone else in your organization send it to the person who will be introducing you before you speak. Most intros are written to boost your perception and make you appear bigger than life, so it appears more humbling if that introduction doesn't come directly from you. Be creative with it.

Your Entrance:

As a *BrandFace*, you are attempting to set the tone of a local celebrity, and this is exactly your moment to do so! Play signature music as you approach the podium. As you'll learn about in the Branding chapter, sonic branding can be powerful. If you don't have a signature sound, consider contacting a nearby recording studio to help you with this task. Otherwise, choose a song or piece of music that you feel represents your brand and will get the audience pumped up. If you plan to use someone else's song beyond this event, you'll most likely need permission to do so, or agree to pay royalty fees. Get creative when choosing a song, not just for the melody but the lyrics as well. If the lyrics say something about you or your brand, it's a great connection.

Your Audio/Visual Presentation:

Simple, graphic-heavy presentations are best. Most people use Power Point or a similar program. The best visual presentations will show one slide every two to three minutes, with minimal text. Graphics and photos are best to represent a thought or make a point. I look at my visuals as a graphic representation of my speech outline. In other words, if I write down one word or phrase to represent each portion of my speech, I try to find a graphic or image that best represents that word or phrase. That way, the slides also serve as a trigger for me about what part of the speech comes next. I also try to utilize video or audio in the presentation whenever possible. This can include anything from client testimonials to event footage or an instructional video explaining a specific product or service in greater detail.

Audience Interaction:
Make sure you interact with your audience throughout the event. This personalizes you even more, and also gives your audience a chance to think about themselves and what they want out of the event. Even if it means simply supplying an index card to all attendees as they enter and requesting that they write down a question about the topic of your talk. This way, no one will feel like a deer in the headlights when you call on them to ask a question. It helps them to be better prepared and more relaxed, and gives them time to think about important questions. Take those questions throughout or at the end of your session. This provides give-and-take moments that can make your audience feel involved.

Test The Equipment:
Much anxiety has been had over technical difficulties. Whenever possible, I try to visit the location where I'll be speaking to scout out the size of the room, audience layout and technical set-up. Where should the screen go? Which audio set-up will work best for the size of the room? Are there sufficient electrical outlets near my computer or projector? Arriving early to an event also gives me time to make sure everything is working properly, from the presentation to the microphone and audio equipment. Finally, I always have an additional copy of my presentation materials on a backup flash drive as a precautionary measure. You might even go one step further and print hand-outs of slide thumbnails just in case the projector malfunctions! Handling these potential challenges in advance can make for a very smooth, professional presentation.

PROMOTING THE EVENT
Sometimes you will be hired to speak at a private event, meaning attendance is by special invitation only. Other times the attendance will be open to the public, and should be promoted to target prospects in a public manner. Here are a few suggestions for getting the most publicity from your talk.

Publicizing a Private Event:
If the event is private, the organization that hired you will take care of the invitations. In this case, it's still important from a *BrandFace* perspective to get some public relations mileage out of your speaking session. Create a press

release about the event and submit it to pertinent media outlets. You'll find more information on press releases in the Public Relations chapter. In addition, use your social media outlets to thank the organization publicly for bringing you on board to speak at their event, and be sure to tag them in your posts. When the event is over, post photos with the company owners and event organizers. This shows courtesy and gratitude, but also accomplishes the need to publicize your work.

Promoting a Public Event:
If the event is open to the public, turn on the charm! Send out a press release, promote shamelessly on social media and send notices about it to your database through email marketing channels. When you promote, focus on what attendees will learn at the event, and the impact it could have on their professional or personal lives. If there are other speakers at this event, contact them and ask their permission to promote them and their content as well. Most often, the other speakers will appreciate this and offer to do the same for you by promoting you to their own networks. The most successful speakers will realize that this approach benefits both parties, and it can help to grow both your networks. Another excellent promotional idea is to shoot a short video announcing your appearance at the upcoming event, and inviting your connections to attend or sign up for the event. Post the video on all your social channels and link to it from your e-newsletter. It's another personal *BrandFace* moment!

SALES OPPORTUNITIES
Opportunities for back of the room sales are limitless if you get creative enough. Most professional speakers have products or services to sell such as books, videos, training programs and consulting services. Here are some ideas for generating revenue from your speaking engagements.

Motivational Posters:
One professional speaker (Dr. Mike Thomson with *It's All About Character*, drmikethomson.com) prints a series of posters and laminated postcards to address child behavior, responsibility and accountability. His 'Good Choice. Poor Choice. My Choice.' tips are designed to assist parents and kids while walking through a decision-making process together based on the questions on the poster. Producing items that call for regular use of a system or process is an excellent way to ensure that your materials are useful in an ongoing manner.

Postcards:
Use postcards to promote the landing page you want your audience to visit when the event is over. Include a special offer on the postcard which should

be strong enough to at least get them to the page, like a price discount on your products, free download of your new e-book or white paper or a promo code to get a sneak peek at your new video. On the landing page, make sure to include a link to your online marketplace where they can purchase all your products and services, and especially a link to sign up for email communication from you. If you have a mobile app, encourage downloads for your app as well.

Books or Mini-Books:
Nothing says expertise like becoming an author. Whether it's a traditional book or a scaled-down promotional mini-book, these are perhaps the best sellers at an event. It's something tangible that your attendees can walk out with, and immediately continue the learning process you set in place during your talk. Consider taking one of your exclusive numbered lists from one of your content sessions (example: Michael's '12 Pillars of Success') and producing a mini-book. They demonstrate a focus on expertise in a specific category and you can claim authorship, even if it's only 50 pages!

E-Books:
Personally, I don't buy very many physical books since I purchased my Amazon Kindle. I prefer reading on the tablet, because I do most of my reading at night, and the ease of use with a tablet backlight and the ability to hold the device and turn pages with literally one finger is a no-brainer. In my opinion, it's a must to develop an e-reader version of any book you create. This will also sell quickly, as the instantaneous download will appeal to those seeking immediate gratification.

CDs, DVDs or Flash Drives:
Basically any audio, video or file storage device will do. These could include audio books, a collection of your educational materials (e-books, how-to guides, tips and advice, etc.) or instructional videos just to name a few.

Promotional Items:
Consider cleverly branded promotional items, like bookmarks with your web address. Think of simple items that people will use almost daily, like USB flash drives (pre-loaded with your content), portable mobile phone and tablet chargers, car chargers, and tablet covers and cases. Consider unique items like yoga mats for fitness buffs or recyclable grocery tote bags for the environmentally conscious.

FOLLOW-UP
Drive Them Online:
When you do any type of talk, it's imperative that you share with your

audience several ways they can connect with you online after the event. I love landing pages for this purpose. For instance, I spoke for the Ohio Newspaper Association and at the end of my talk, I promoted a customized landing page which gave them additional information and promoted my online training series for media sales professionals. The page allowed them to download '10 Ways to Build Fans & Followers' as well as view a free Idea Camp, an integrated campaign approach they could immediately sell to one of their newspaper clients. It also allowed them to sign up to receive training updates, so any time a new campaign idea was added to the training platform, they would be notified. Lastly, it provided a link to the training program itself, so they could explore and sign up. The possibilities are numerous, and the main goal should be capturing contact information, which eventually leads to sales.

Follow-Up:
As part of your speaking negotiations, always ask for a copy of the attendee roster, including email addresses. If the business hiring you is hesitant to provide this, offer to email the attendees something of value on the business' behalf after the event, or to include something from the business into your landing page as a follow-up (link to a loan application or link to sign up for their company newsletter). That way, the audience receives only the information pertaining to the event in your follow-up, and the content is also tied to the business that hired you. Follow up with a personal thank you to all attendees. If the group was small, consider using vSnap videos as an individual follow-up (see the Video chapter for more information about vSnap). These are extremely personal and powerful videos!

——————————— **Ron's Message** ———————————

I've done a lot of public speaking over the years. In fact, my booklet, '25 Things I Believe' actually came from a speaking engagement I did at The Columbus State College for their Business Program's Leadership Speaker Series. Within the first couple of weeks after I began working with Tonya, she stumbled upon that video on our YouTube channel and felt the content was perfect for a short book. And as luck would have it, we were just celebrating our 25th anniversary, so everything fell right into place with those 25 topics of advice.

I feel right at home at a podium. In fact, I feel like part of my job is teaching. Each week, I speak at sales meetings in an attempt to motivate our team, and they always seem to respond well to it. I've always just had a knack for inspiring and motivating people.

I'd strongly suggest public speaking to anyone who is a BrandFace. It's one of the most effective ways to establish your credibility. Prepare a unique speech that you can deliver over and over. Let it become your signature speech. As long as it's coming from the heart and is relatable to your audience, you'll win them over. People want realism.

Chapter 16:

KILLER

COLLATERAL MATERIALS

Collateral materials are designed to reinforce the marketing and advertising of a company or brand. They include items such as business cards, letterhead, flyers, brochures, presentations, catalogs, point-of-purchase displays and more. The purpose of this chapter is to help you understand how to incorporate your *BrandFace* image and expertise into these pieces in order to maintain brand consistency. As with many other topics in this book, the options are so numerous, they could literally fill another book. But here are some suggestions for the most popular types of collateral.

Business Cards:
There has been much debate about whether to include your photo on business cards. I believe it's another *BrandFace* moment which will enable others to remember you not only by your title, but by your face as well, so I vote 'Yes'. Real estate agents and insurance agents have been using this tactic successfully for years. Your business card should reflect a professional image with a warm, friendly smile. Not too corporate looking, but this is certainly not the collateral piece to display a very casual or creative photo. Though increasingly the electronic version of your business card (v-card) is most used, your traditional printed business card is still one of the pieces which may remain in the hands of your prospects, peers and customers for a long time. Think about unique ways to use the back of your business card. A quote from you or a testimonial from a high profile client will be more memorable than just your logo. Physicians often use the back of their cards as appointment reminders. Add a QR code (learn more about these in the Mobile Marketing chapter) that links to a simple sign-up form for your newsletter, or a promotion such as 'text HEALTHY to 01234 to receive a coupon for a free protein bar'. Think of the different ways your business card can be used to boost sign-ups, fans, followers and store traffic. If you own a landscape nursery, think about customized seed packets for a business card. USB flash drives come in all shapes and sizes, can be custom printed and would be another option to serve as a unique business card. Whatever you choose, make sure it's different from others in your industry, and represents what is unique about you and your business.

Brochures:
A company brochure is generally a brief presentation of your company's

point of differentiation, products and services. Many companies produce a different brochure for each product or service as well. Some options for design might include a stand-up image of yourself on the brochure, with a quote next to your image about the attributes of the product or service—or a signature tagline from you (which is also used in your advertising campaigns). If you feel those options aren't a precise fit, one tactic we use is to put your *BrandFace* photo on the back panel with your company contact information. Either way you go, just one image of you on the piece should suffice.

Postcards:

Postcards (or other direct mail options) can be an excellent targeting vehicle if you are interested in reaching a specific geographic area, or even based on demographics such as income levels, household values, etc. They are used very successfully by the home improvement industry, especially. Postcards are meant to get right to the point about a specific topic or offer. At a glance, the prospect should be able to tell the purpose of the message or campaign. Bullet points or phrases are better than paragraphs of text. Include an image of yourself on the front or back, but generally not both sides. Designing a postcard is similar to designing a banner ad. You have to be precise and to the point. Because you have limited space, it forces you to be specific and to consider your messaging carefully. Powerful headlines are essential with any type of advertising, but especially so with limited space.

Magazines:

I love the idea of a company magazine, a signature showcase piece designed to highlight all the important facets, divisions, products, services, goals, etc. of your business. Instead of a full size magazine, consider the more popular hand-out size such as a mini-magazine or booklet. There are no strict guidelines on size. I've seen them as small as a postcard and slightly larger than a greeting card. When you produce a piece that focuses on everything your company provides, consider using colored side tabs or page edges to separate the different categories or divisions. I especially like the idea of your *BrandFace* image on the inside front and/or back cover, next to your mission statement.

Thank You Cards:

Everyone should have personalized thank you cards, and most especially a *BrandFace*. The hand-written word makes even more of an impact in today's high tech world. Put your photo on the card cover or inside, but don't pre-print your written signature on the cards. That's a great online tactic, but if you take the time to write a thank you card, include an actual signature as well. If you're known for your humor or telling stories about growing up in the family business, you might put a funny childhood photo on the card instead. If you have a signature saying, you can order cards that are equipped with audio which plays the moment they're opened. If you're a real estate agent, consider a thank you card with your full standing image next to a front door that says 'Welcome to your dream home' on the cover, and 'Thank you for choosing us to open the door' on the inside.

Ron's Message

The first thing I'd like to mention when it comes to collateral materials is the logo that goes on every piece of marketing we do. When I first started working with Tonya, I knew our logo needed a facelift. At the time, my logo had my actual photo in it, and that was on all our company vehicles, signage, etc. But we knew it was outdated and needed a fresh new look. We didn't only discuss the look of the logo, we discussed the long term plan of the company and the impact that would have on our logo. Since I was the face of the brand, it was vitally important to keep some representation of me in the logo. However, we needed to make sure that I stopped aging in that logo in order to fulfill our long term plan, which was to eventually have a Basement Doctor in every city in the U.S. We decided to go with a sketch of my face, but instead of being an exaggerated caricature, it was an actual likeness, an image that was immediately recognizable as me—beard, ball cap and all. It's sort of like Colonel Sanders on the Kentucky Fried Chicken logo.

Regarding the individual collateral pieces we use every day, I think the most impressive thing we've done is to develop a system for new product arrivals. When new products come in, our staff knows immediately what kind of information and photos we need in order to launch it, and we put those through a predetermined system. Within hours, we have collateral materials ready to go. It's saved us so much time to have those collateral templates on hand.

And yes, we create all of our collateral materials with our own in-house marketing team. They understand our products, systems and philosophies better than anyone. This also allows us the flexibility to make revisions on the fly to accommodate any last minute changes.

Example E: Ron's personal business card
Example F: Consumer's Guide Brochure
Example G: Spring Newsletter
Example H: Fall Newsletter

Chapter 17:

VIDEO MADE
THE BRANDFACE® STAR

The most versatile form of content, videos are powerful marketing tools. When you can't be in front of a prospect one-to-one, they're the next best thing to being there. An estimated 93% of marketers used video for online marketing, sales or communications purposes in 2013 (Source: Web Video Marketing Council, ReelSEO and Flimp Media, 2013). Increasingly, we find ourselves suggesting and utilizing more online video for our client's campaigns. As a *BrandFace*, it's the perfect way for your prospects and customers to connect with you and learn about your expertise and personality.

My real estate client recently made a very insightful statement. He said, "I'd love to personally communicate with every customer. But as my company grows, that becomes more difficult, and my customers will increasingly deal with my sales staff and agents. Being a *BrandFace* has given me a way to stay in front of those clients as the face of my business in other ways." I couldn't agree more. Just so happens, this client's marketing strategy is loaded with video.

VIDEO BENEFITS
Here are several reasons I love video as a form of effective communication.

Taking Offline to Online:
All forms of media can instantly direct and connect consumers to online video across multiple devices. Remember to use all forms of your advertising to accomplish this goal. If you're doing print ads, display a QR code linked to video. If you're using radio or TV, drive them online with a URL that's easy to recall & spell, and connects prospects to your videos for maximum impact.

On Demand:
Online video is available anytime, anywhere, on any internet-capable device. Even IPTV (Internet Protocol TV) options such as Netflix, Hulu and Amazon are available from these devices. In fact, it's estimated that globally, consumer internet video traffic will be 69 percent of all consumer internet traffic in 2017 (Source: Cisco®Visual Networking Index, 2013).

Emotional Connection:

Video not only helps branding efforts, it provides a personal, emotional connection. If you've seen someone in a video--then meet them in person--you feel like you already know them. Plus, a whopping 57% of consumers say that product videos make them more confident in a purchase and less likely to return an item (Source: Mediapost, 2013).

Improved Search Rankings:

You probably already know that the number one search engine in the world is Google. But did you know that YouTube is number two? This tells you a lot about the power of video today. We see more and more search returns for video on the first page of Google, even ahead of traditional web pages. You'll find advice all over the web about utilizing YouTube for its search benefits. Embedding your YouTube videos on your website can definitely enhance search engine rankings.

More Qualified Leads:

Using video as a sales tool to help your prospects learn more about your products/services can ensure that they are more educated before you meet one on one, thus producing better qualified prospects. Not only does it help your customer learn more, it positions your brand as synonymous with expertise and quality.

Higher Engagement Rates:

51.9% of marketing professionals worldwide cite video as the type of content with the best ROI (Source: CopyPress, 2013 State of Content Marketing Study, Feb 12, 2013). When consumers interact with video, they tend to stay on your site longer, and spend more time with your content.

VIDEO TYPES

Video topic ideas are limitless, but there are some stand-outs which I believe are necessary for marketing your business. Here are a few types of videos I'd recommend you have in your collection.

Business Intro:

This video introduces you and your business and shares how you got started, what you specialize in, who benefits from your products/services and what makes you unique.

Educational:

These videos generally feature products and services. This gives you the opportunity to showcase your products visually, or provide a clear illustration or explanation of your services. Especially if a particular service is complicated to explain, a video can simplify that. In a perfect world, it would be best to have a separate video for each major product or service.

Philanthropy:

When it comes to philanthropic efforts, it's always best to take the approach of promoting the good works of the charities you support versus your own. The sheer fact that you are the provider of this type of video says a lot. Take time to explain why you support those organizations, and then give a brief synopsis of what each does. If the charity already has video footage you can use, weave that into your video. If not, make sure to grab footage of events that you are involved in throughout the year (which you should be doing anyway!). Don't forget to recognize your own staff members who participate throughout the year. If this video is focused on local charity organizations or issues and the good deeds of your employees, you know you're doing it right!

Event:

Whether it's your own company event or an event that you attend or sponsor, this content can highlight your involvement in the community. If you are speaking to a group, grab the footage. Find out what your attendees think about an event by getting their reaction on video as they exit. At the very least, an event video can serve as documentation and serve as a benchmark for improvement in your next event.

Instructional:

Any time a product or service requires explanation or step-by-step instructions, it's an opportunity to become an authority on the subject. This can range from installation of a product to explanation of the complicated new healthcare law. One of the most popular video types for explanation or instruction is an animated sketch video. It uses drawing and animation to make a point.

Training:

Training videos are an excellent way to provide educational insight for your employees, vendors and customers alike. Instead of continually repeating instructions for a task, shoot an instructional video *once* and it can serve as a resource moving forward. I use a tool called SnagIt that allows you to do video screen recordings for quick and simple training videos. Unless something major changes with your process, systems or tools, only minor future updates are necessary. As a *BrandFace*, I suggest that you shoot a brief intro and outro for each video. Each time your viewers see these training videos, it's another branding connection.

Tour:

If you have an impressive facility and would like your customers to see the place where all the work is completed, a video tour is a great way to accomplish that. It's also a personal way to introduce your staff members to your customers, especially those customers who live outside your market and don't often get a chance to visit.

Testimonial:

The only thing more powerful than a *BrandFace* sharing the attributes of their business is a customer testimonial. Happy customers create more customers. After every completed project, ask your customers to share their experience with your company on video.

Promotional:

If you have a special, limited time offer to extend, short form videos that are featured on social platforms are great for this purpose. My advice is to only showcase these on social media when you are offering something *free*, with no strings attached! Otherwise, it breaks most social media rules regarding cheesy sales pitches. Consider a personal invitation to try a new product or receive a service free in exchange for customer feedback.

Bloopers!

Marketing shouldn't be all business and no fun. Every *BrandFace* has a unique personality, and the most humorous side of us often appears when we're *attempting* to be serious, but find ourselves making mistakes. A bloopers reel is an excellent way of showcasing your lighter side, and sharing more of the human element in your marketing.

Introductory or Thank You Videos:

I use an online video tool called vSnap for sending short, personal introduction and thank you videos. It's available in desktop, tablet or mobile versions, and allows you to use your web camera to shoot a one-minute video and immediately email it to the recipient. It's a very personal, one-to-one tool and should be utilized that way. I use it after every initial meeting with a client, and have also used it to introduce myself to new prospects. I've been in several meetings where the first fifteen minutes was spent listening to my prospects talk about how impressed they were to receive a vSnap video from me!

Live Stream Videos:

Broadcasting a live event can be a powerful way to engage your customer. Events should be at least a few hours long in order to attract mass viewers, but live broadcasting performs best when the event takes place over several days. This is a creative way to engage your customer. One of my clients recently attended a Home & Garden Show and had a staff member follow him with a video camera as he did brief interviews with other vendors. This was a brilliant move, as it positioned him as an industry leader while showcasing other vendors, some of whom were his competitors. Imagine streaming this kind of video live from the home show for the entire weekend. Live streaming platforms range from free, such as Google Hangouts, to paid services like Ustream and Livestream.

VIDEO TIPS

Here are some tips which will make your video more memorable and consistent with your *BrandFace* concept.

Overlays:

Use graphic and text overlays on top of your video which might include your name, title, business logo and contact information. You can leave the overlays up for the entire video, or just include them at the beginning and the end.

Presence:

You don't have to be a talking head throughout the entire video. Make an appearance at the beginning of the video to set a welcoming tone, and again at the end as a wrap-up. In between, you can use photos or other footage with your voiceover. This achieves the *BrandFace* connection you need while keeping the viewer visually engaged.

Embedded Links:

YouTube allows you to link images in your videos. For instance, if you're selling a book, you can include an image of the book in your video and link that image to your website. You can also take the entire final frame of a video and do the same. Utilize these links to take your prospects where you want them to go.

CHANNEL CUSTOMIZATION

There are multiple video platforms, but the one I recommend most is YouTube. Since YouTube is owned by Google, it certainly can't hurt you in the search department. To get the most from your YouTube channel, here are some suggestions for strategy and customization:

Images:

Customize your channel with a channel icon and cover art. Use one of your professional *BrandFace* photos in either option, but not both. If you choose to put your picture in the cover photo, use your logo as the smaller profile picture. Make sure you remain consistent with the look and feel of your brand, using one of your signature images as the backdrop in the cover photo.

About:
Take the time to include a short bio about your channel. This should always include your name and the name of your business for both branding and search purposes. Describe the videos on your channel and name your products and services in this description.

Playlists:
Segment your videos into playlists by topic. For instance, consider playlists such as About (you or your company), Products & Services, How-To's, Events, Testimonials, etc. Some people ask if they should include their TV commercials on their YouTube channel. My gut response is that people come to YouTube to be educated, informed or entertained, not for a commercial sales pitch. However, from a sheer search standpoint, it doesn't hurt to upload those and put them in a separate playlist called TV Commercials. At least it's transparent.

Custom Thumbnails:
Each video that you upload comes with three options for a thumbnail or small still image which will appear on your channel and anywhere your video is embedded. But did you ever upload a video just to find that all three snapshots of you in the thumbnail images were displaying a horrifying frozen facial expression? I certainly have. And that's no image for a *BrandFace*, right? Fortunately, you can fix that. First, go into your Video Manager, then Channel Settings. In your account status, you should see an option to verify your account. This is as simple as entering your phone number so YouTube can send you a code via text, which you can then enter into the page. Once your account is verified, you'll then be able to upload a custom thumbnail. You'll see this option when you attempt to edit any video. It displays just under the three auto-generated thumbnails on the edit page. You can choose to create an image to represent your video, such as a title image or scroll through your existing video and get a screen grab that looks less than horrifying. Once you do that, you can use just about any graphic editing program and crop out the new video player image. Then just upload the new image via the custom thumbnail upload option.

Comments:
Allowing your visitors to post comments about your videos is a great way to keep the communication flow open. However, the comments area of websites is often open to hackers and people with harmful intentions. My

advice is to allow comments, but based only on your approval. If you set your account to allow comments with approval only, you'll be able to quickly preview the comment and either delete or approve it by way of a notification email.

Channel Trailer:
You have the option to upload a video describing your channel, which should encourage others to subscribe to it or feature it. I suggest producing a separate video for this purpose rather than attempting to re-purpose an existing video. However, when that isn't an option, use your 'About' video, which should feature the story behind you and your company.

Subscriptions:
You can subscribe to other YouTube channels if you find a channel with helpful or interesting material. When you do this, their videos will appear in your subscription area. And when they upload a new video, you will be notified (as long as your notification permissions are set to notify you). The advantage of this is the convenience of having their content at your fingertips, especially if you rely on that content to create your own. For instance, you might want to subscribe to your vendor's channels so you can see their new product videos as they are posted.

Add Links:
At the bottom right corner of your cover art, you have the ability to add four different links to your websites or other social platforms. Add these links through the 'About' tab of your channel, and they will appear as icons or with brief descriptions. Since you're limited to four, choose the four links that best represent a connection to you based on the videos you've chosen to feature on your channel.

Featured Channels:
Adding other YouTube channels as featured channels is an excellent way to strengthen and develop relationships with strategic partners. Add the channels of your vendors and promotional partners and ask that they do the same for you. It's one more way to grow both of your networks.

Descriptions and Tagging:
When you upload your videos, take the time to write a custom description of each video and tag each of them properly, using keywords that a prospect might use to search for the specific content your video contains. This is a critical step in the effort to achieve higher search rankings and attain more views. Always include your own name and business name in the video description.

Promotion:

Each time you upload a new video, your channel subscribers will be notified. For all others in your network, make sure to post the link to the new video across all your social platforms. As a *BrandFace*, it's a great idea to add a short sentence with a personal touch each time you post a new video link. Consider something like "Learn about our brand new product line which can save you thousands in energy bills. I've personally been searching for a product like this since I started this business in 1975".

SHOOTING YOUR OWN VIDEO

Investing in video can be a powerful way to communicate, but it can also be costly. Ultimately, having someone on your staff who can at least shoot great video (and leave the editing to the pros) is ideal. For a relatively small investment and a little bit of practice, you can produce simple photo slide videos, client testimonial videos, meet the team videos and more. I've compiled some recommendations here to help you set up your own in-house video studio. These are simply recommendations based on my experience, and you are free to choose whichever equipment or software you feel best fits your skill level.

Cameras:

There are many HD video cameras on the market today which would be suitable for your needs. I'd suggest you visit your local electronics store and explain that you're looking for a camera to shoot your own videos in both indoor (with a green or white screen) and outdoor locations. Look for a camera with audio jacks, so you can plug in an external microphone for better audio quality, as well as a USB connection for transferring the video to your computer. Generally, you can expect to pay between $250 and $350 for a decent camera. Don't get lost in the camera-snob reviews. You're not shooting HD video for TV or a Hollywood blockbuster. These are short, disposable, digital videos for use on the web. Good lighting and a simple camera is all you need.

Digital Voice Recorder:

Have you ever watched a great video, but felt the quality was subpar due to poor audio? It happens a lot. For price and simplicity, I'd recommend purchasing a portable digital audio recorder. These usually range in price from $30-$40. In addition, buy a lapel microphone, which can increase the audio quality tenfold. Make sure it includes an audio jack for an external microphone and a USB connection for transferring files to your computer.

Video Editing:

First, unless you have someone on staff who can edit video, I'd recommend leaving the editing to the professionals. You can cut down on your video costs greatly just by shooting your own video in-house, then uploading for your editing pros to finish the job. However, if you do have someone who can edit video, Adobe Premiere Elements is the editing software we use, and I've found it fairly easy to learn. It includes lots of bells and whistles even for the stripped-down version, and produces some pretty slick video for a relatively small investment. There are numerous how-to videos on YouTube for Premiere Elements as well. You can purchase the software online at Adobe.com for approximately $100. Be sure to select the right software for your operating system (Mac vs. PC). Also, check your local office supply store for sales, particularly around back to school time.

Lighting:

It's tempting to want to skip on this investment, but the best quality videos require good audio and lighting. TubeTape.net has continuous, soft box lighting kits around $200.00. Additionally there are hundreds of tutorial videos on lighting your subject on YouTube, which will give any video you shoot that extra pop of professionalism.

Green Screen:

Shooting video with a green screen and good lighting can provide a tremendous amount of flexibility with video backgrounds. A green screen, which is just a large piece of chroma-key green cloth (usually muslin fabric) will allow you or your editor the ability to drop your storefront, logo or other scene in the background. Premiere Elements has built-in settings to help you remove the green screen and replace with any background you can imagine. TubeTape.net also has green screens starting in the $20 range.

Stock Video & Photos:

Sometimes it's necessary to use stock video footage or photos to achieve the look you want. Videohive.net is an excellent resource for animated graphics, animated transitions and various types of stock video. Fotolia.com is a resource for stock photos and video. Add that extra kick to your video production. Each site allows you to bank money and debit against the balance as you go. You only restock when your funds run low, so it's an excellent 'pay as you go' option.

Internal Shooting:

You really don't need a ton of space. A spare office or a dedicated area of a larger space can become the permanent home for your in-house video shoots. You can even use areas like the conference room, or other rooms that may not be used as frequently as a person's office or common area. The main thing to consider is whether there is sufficient room to move your lighting and video equipment around without tripping over wires and cables.

Starter Investment:

For the sake of argument, let's assume you're starting with nothing, and need all the basic video equipment, including editing software and a few stock images or video elements for your first video production. Here's a list using average prices to give you an idea of your initial investment for video.

Camera	$350
Audio Recorder	$40
Lapel Microphone	$30
Editing Software	$120
Lighting Kit	$200
Green Screen	$30
Videohive.net (1-2 stock video elements)	$30
Fotolia.com (3-4 stock images)	$30
TOTAL	**$790**

Video Hosting:

Finally, I recommend hosting your videos on external sites so that you can save on bandwidth charges, while taking advantage of additional exposure offered through these highly traveled video sites. These sites include You Tube, Blip.tv, Vimeo and others. These sites not only host your videos, they track use of the video, and provide embedding options for using the video elsewhere (like your campaign site, website and social media platforms) or privacy options to keep access to a select few. YouTube is where we store all our videos, mostly due to the immense traffic and search benefits.

–––––––––––––– **Ron's Message** ––––––––––––––

If I had to choose one thing that really catapulted The Basement Doctor brand to fame, I'd say it was video. The very first time we ran TV ads, I began to notice the response. It was like the local celebrity effect Tonya talks about. I became known as a trusted figure. People felt like they already knew me and there seemed to be a familiarity with our company. It was truly a trust vehicle for me. Here was this guy, looking very approachable, standing next to his company truck and delivering an honest message to his customers. "If you have a wet, nasty, dirty crawl space or basement, we have affordable solutions to give you a drier, cleaner, healthier, safer and more energy efficient home". That message resonated and still does to this day.

We have literally hundreds of videos on our YouTube channel today. One of the most viewed to date is a video of me on a local TV station being interviewed by the news anchor inside the basement of someone's home. I was showing people how we tackle specific problems in a home setting. It was an educational piece that brought a lot of value to our customer base. We continue to do lots of those today.

Example I: 'Meet Ron Greenbaum' video
Example J: Ron's Bloopers Video

Chapter 18:

AUDIO—

THE THEATRE OF THE MIND

Since video has become so widely popular online, both in terms of creating and consuming, it seems as though audio has taken a back seat. This chapter will make the case for quite the opposite! People consume content in various ways. Some prefer to read, some to listen, others to view. It has often been referred to as 'theatre of the mind', meaning the lack of visual components leave details open to interpretation, which can be a powerful thing in marketing. All you need to do is think about your favorite music in order to understand that concept. I explain the power of sonic branding in the Branding chapter. Music can mean different things to each of us. We think different thoughts and see different visuals in our mind based on our individual experiences with regard to sound. Audio is a perfect companion for people who multi-task because you don't have to view a video screen, book or e-reader to consume it. It can just play in the background while you're working, exercising, etc. It's a quick and easy way to capture your *BrandFace* content, as well. Some of us communicate best with the spoken word rather than writing our thoughts.

AUDIO BENEFITS
Audio as content should be part of every *BrandFace* strategy. If I haven't already convinced you of its power, here are a few more reasons to consider.

Voice Recognition:
Have you ever been in public and recognized a voice from across the room? Our sense of hearing is powerful. We remember tones, inflections and pitch in someone's voice. It's a signature trait just like our fingerprint. As a *BrandFace*, your voice is one of the most important tools in your marketing arsenal. It not only has a unique sound, it demonstrates your authenticity and sincerity as much as your facial expressions and nonverbal gestures.

Ease of Production:
No cameras, no lighting. Just you and a recorder. It doesn't matter what you wear or how you look. It just matters how you communicate with words. I encourage people who are comfortable doing video to stick with it, because you can utilize both the visual medium as well as the audio. In fact, in most cases you can take the audio track from the video and use it separately, giving you two mediums by which to communicate. But if you're anxious about

doing video or you just prefer audio's ease of production, audio is the perfect choice. Good quality microphones are available for minimal investment, and there are many free audio editing tools available online (Audacity is one that we use).

Multi-Use:
You can create audio content once and use it in multiple ways. Transcribe it as a blog post, article or e-book. Separate your audio into smaller segments or sound bites and use them as multiple podcasts. Extract quotes or sayings from your recordings and make them into a promotional mini-book. Transcribe your interviews and submit them as content for local news sites. Once your thoughts are recorded, there is almost no end to their usefulness.

AUDIO TYPES
Podcasts:
We should probably start this section of the chapter by defining podcasting. There are multiple and varied definitions of the term podcast. The simplest definition is 'a digital audio or video file available for automatic download and/or playing on a computer or digital audio device'. When podcasting first came on the scene, it was purely audio-focused. Video was applied to the term later; however, most people still recognize the term to apply exclusively to audio. Podcasts can encompass all formats of audio, from short tutorials to interviews and much more. In fact, any of the examples listed here would technically qualify as a podcast. Podcasts are available on individual websites and through platforms as large as iTunes, in virtually every category imaginable.

Online Radio Shows:
Have you ever considered hosting your own radio show? Radio broadcasts are one of the most effective means for establishing expertise. I'm speaking of online radio options, specifically (you'll find more information on terrestrial radio in the Traditional Marketing chapter). There are multiple online platforms which allow you to launch your own online radio station. Although the audience can be minimal compared to a traditional radio station, online talk radio audiences are often much more targeted because they are actively seeking your content online. This means more potential for meaningful interaction with your prospects and customers. A couple of popular platforms are Blog Talk Radio & Spreaker. Both platforms allow you to host a live call-in radio show or simply pre-record your show and make it available as a podcast. Their radio shows feature experts in all arenas, including politics, self-improvement, cars, religion, health and fitness, music and much more. If you've never tried this approach, I'd recommend you start by podcasting rather than live streaming. This gives you the opportunity

to work through any bugs and to make sure your audio quality is good, as sometimes live streams can have hiccups when it comes to audio quality. Both Blog Talk Radio and Spreaker also have built-in tools which allow you to upload and edit your audio with music tracks and sound effects.

Audio Books:
Have you noticed that most famous authors today record their own audio books? Especially if your subject is about you and your business or industry, wouldn't it be much more personal to have that content read aloud in your own voice? Audio has long been considered one of the most personal mediums, and I can't think of a more personal *BrandFace* approach than an audio version of your book featuring your voice.

Teleconferencing:
Video conferencing is certainly the most talked about and utilized formats when it comes to online sales and communications, but millions of dollars are still being made today in the world of teleconferencing (a telephone conference between two or more people). It's a personal, effective way to express yourself to an audience of one or thousands. Direct marketers use these to provide details behind a product or service, share powerful stories and convince followers to become rabid fans and paid customers, all through the power of audio.

AUDIO IDEAS
On-Hold System:
Always put customer service first, and pick up the phone as quickly as possible. But for those rare times when you a customer must wait, your voice is what they should hear. Record the on-hold message for your phone system. Think of creative ways to interject your brand or promote new products and services to those on hold. Use your company jingle in addition to your own voice. Make your messages brief, because no one likes to be on hold for long!

Audio Blog Posts:
As mentioned at the beginning of this chapter, people consume content in various ways. Take your existing blog posts and read them aloud for an alternate audio version. For those who prefer audio (especially since we can play audio in the background while we're doing other things), a different content format might be appreciated. You might also find audio to be an easier (and faster) means of recording your content for your blog.

Interviews:
Some of the most powerful interviews I've heard were on the radio. During

video interviews, we're often so focused on how someone looks or the background of the video that we don't always pay attention to the most important part—what they say. Audio interviews are much simpler to conduct than video interviews, as well. A small digital audio recorder is all you need for great sound quality.

FAQ's or Five Questions:
Any *BrandFace* struggles with time constraints. Recording your frequently asked questions and answers via audio can be done almost anywhere. No camera or lighting is needed, and your audio answers inject more personality than just producing a downloadable document with the same information. One of my clients answers five questions in each podcast and posts them monthly. He loves the simplicity and speed of audio.

Audio Tweets:
Imagine a different twist on a tweet. Very few people tweet audio recordings, and it can provide one more way to stand out. Consider a simple idea such as recording quotes. We're often moved or inspired by quotes that we read in various places. Our friends post them on Facebook or Instagram, they're printed on collateral materials and even sprinkled throughout websites. Record the quotes yourself and link to the recording in your tweet. State the quote, the source and your brief thoughts on why that quote resonates with you. There are several apps available for audio tweets. It's a simple way to connect on a different level than most, and is just one more way to brand your unique voice.

Background Music:
Audio is about far more than your own voice. Music is one of the most impactful ways to connect with your audience. Learn more about sonic branding in the Branding chapter. Consider the music you play in your office, on your on-hold system, on your website and in your jingle. If you use music on your website, keep in mind the advice from the Video chapter and do *not* set it to auto-play. These are your signature sounds, and can be so powerful in creating a feeling about you and your business. Don't take these choices lightly. Consider sounds that will resonate with your audience in a way that is meaningful and purposeful.

Content Teasers:
Record snippets of content from your new book or e-book as a teaser. Make sure you give people enough information in the teaser so they feel their time spent listening was worthwhile, but include a call to action such as 'for more on this subject, visit [website] and download my e-book free!

Testimonials:

Let's face it—written testimonials are just plain boring. And they're much more powerful in video or audio form. Since audio is so much simpler to capture, keep a digital audio recorder with you at all times, and capture feedback from your customers virtually anywhere! You can post a link next to the written testimonials on your website and even include these audio bits in your social media posts.

Trivia:

Record a trivia question each week and post it to social media so your network can respond. This means they have a chance to hear your voice every single week, and in an unusual way that they will likely remember. When you record the trivia question, remind fans and followers to submit their guesses. Consider offering a gift card for a free coffee each week for the first person who responds first with the correct answer. It's a creative and inexpensive way to enhance your brand with audio, and reward your fans and followers at the same time.

Ron's Message

I've been told I have a very memorable voice, and I've actually been recognized many times by my voice alone. I've heard, "I thought that sounded like you" numerous times over the years!

But the most memorable thing about the power of audio is what a catchy jingle can do for you. Ours end with the words, 'The Basement Doctor's On The Job'. It's a catchy tune that truly caught me by surprise when I witnessed its effects. Whenever I'm in public, especially at an event, people of all ages come up to me and start singing this jingle. We even captured one of those impromptu moments on video during a local parade!

As a result of this reaction, I make it a point to use that jingle in all our radio ads, TV ads and web videos. I feel as though it's part of the fiber of the brand, and our marketing wouldn't seem complete without it.

Example K: All Sump Pumps Fail radio commercial

Chapter 19:

CAMPAIGN SITES
WITH LASER BEAM FOCUS

A campaign site, often called a micro site, is a *focused* web page designed to fulfill a specific call to action for an advertising campaign. Campaign sites can be used for virtually any targeted purpose. They're generally used when you want to promote a specific event, product or service, promotion, initiative or to focus on a target consumer. In my opinion, they are one of the most powerful ways to communicate a campaign message. Here are some reasons to consider campaign sites:

BENEFITS
Focus:
The goal of a campaign site is to isolate all the important information in one place and make it easier for your customers to find. It's important to note, however, that a campaign site is never intended to take the place of your main website. It's designed to serve as a 'campaign stop', and always has links to your main website so your prospects can explore further once they have responded to the specific call to action for your advertising campaign.

Streamlines Search:
I'm often asked why we use campaign sites rather than just driving prospects to your main website. You can, but the goal is to make it very easy for the prospect to find exactly what they heard/saw/read about in response to your advertising. After all, your main website has information about every facet of your business, and very often it just takes too many clicks to get to the information which sparked their interest. Additionally, sometimes you don't have access to change your homepage or cannot change it quickly enough to meet the campaign time table. And if the information your customers seek isn't obvious and accessible from the home page, your advertising dollars are wasted. There are also times when your main website URL (or domain name) is hard to spell, which can throw a serious wrench into an otherwise wonderful campaign.

Easy to Remember:
When should you use a standalone URL (ex: FordSpecialOffer.com)? These are often called vanity URLs. When it's catchy, easy to remember and easy to spell, it can draw a lot of qualified traffic (ex: MothersDayContest.com). It says what it is. Removing the intimidation factor is another option. For

instance, would you be more likely to respond to "visit SmithToyota.com to see this month's specials" OR "go to ToyotaCash.com to download your instant $500 coupon"? Using something like ToyotaCash.com completely removes the feeling of being 'sold' and replaces it with a feeling of 'providing a service'.

Measurement:

Every campaign should have some form of measurement. If your advertising drives prospects to your main website, those measurements can often get lost. You're not sure exactly which advertising platforms are working because they're all pointing to the same place. Campaigns sites are great for tracking. Assume you're an HVAC company doing a contest giveaway for a new air conditioning system. If you reserve the domain name CoolContest.com, you can measure the people who visit this site as a result of (only) the contest. You can even take it one step further and measure different advertising outlets by using different extensions of the URL (example: CoolContest.com/radio or CoolContest.com/TV).

CAMPAIGN SITE ELEMENTS

There are different goals for different campaigns, but for planning purposes, here are some elements that are included in almost every successful campaign site.

Single Focus:

The focus of the website must be a single topic. Don't mix your message or promote other areas of your business just because you have the real estate to do so. If the goal of your campaign is to promote your automotive service department, do not include a button encouraging visitors to check out the new Ford Focus or worse yet, view your entire inventory. You will already have one link back to your main site, and if they're that curious, they will click it and explore. Stay true to the goal of promoting your services. For instance, we worked with Wide Open West (a cable provider) to promote their *On Demand* movie selections. The campaign site focused solely on a *BrandFace* movie reviews approach for that specific product line, with a link back to their main site for more information on upcoming new releases.

Powerful Headline:

Your campaign site should always incorporate a headline that immediately informs visitors of its purpose. Look no further than the sites which are promoted on infomercials. Take for instance the Flex Seal site, a spray-on product that coats, seals and stops leaks. When you first get to the site, the headline at the top reads, "The easy way to coat, seal and stop leaks fast!" If you are using your campaign site for contest registration, state the name and purpose of your contest in the headline.

Highlights:
In one or two short paragraphs or bullets, explain why the visitor should be interested, what their participation means to *them* and what they need to do in order to take action. Once visitors see the headline, this is the part they usually read next if their interest is piqued.

Video:
It's probably no surprise that the most successful campaign sites include some type of video. It's the best way to allow prospects to see your face and hear your voice. Depending upon your campaign goal, you can explain a service, educate visitors about an industry misconception, share the top reasons to purchase a brand new product and countless other uses.

Calls to Action:
You must have a single focus for the site, but that doesn't mean you can't have more than one call to action related to that specific focus. For example, a landing page promoting a new training system can have several goals: view the education video about the training, sign up for the monthly training newsletter, get new fans and followers on social media or download your new training tips app. As long as all these calls to action are exclusive to your training system focus, it's perfectly acceptable to have several. However, the *main* call to action should be front and center. So if your most desired action is to capture the email addresses of your visitors, you'll want to make sure the newsletter sign-up stands out.

Opt-In:
Permission-based marketing is not only good practice, it's the law (see more in the Email Marketing chapter). Each time you ask for contact information, make sure you ask permission to add the visitor to your contact list. This is usually in the form of a checkbox opt-in on your registration form. It might say something like, "Yes, please sign me up to receive exclusive offers and event notices!" When the visitor checks that box, they have opted in to receive one-to-one communication from you. Treat that person like a VIP. Be sure to send them *only* the information they signed up to receive, and make sure it's relevant and purposeful.

Link to Main Site:
As mentioned earlier, always include a link to your main website somewhere on the landing page. It doesn't need to be too obvious, just make it available. I know you will be tempted to make it large or even turn it into a graphic button, but refrain from turning your focused campaign site into a scattered

mess.

Tracking:

Google Analytics is a free tracking tool which will allow you to measure your campaign ROI. If you don't already have an account, they're free to set up and relatively easy to connect to your site. Have your web administrator add the tracking code to each page of your campaign site and you'll be able to track your total visits, unique visitors, bounce rate, time spent on the page and more. You can also see where your traffic is coming from (referring URL's). If you are utilizing more than one page to measure each advertising outlet, you will be able to track those visits as well.

WHY THEY'RE IMPORTANT

I receive lots of questions about campaign sites and landing pages with regard to third party sites such as media outlet websites. Many advertisers are approached by media outlets to advertise on their websites or even have their campaign site live on the media outlet's website. On the surface, it seems to make sense. After all, the media outlet website gets more visitors, right? But my question is not the quantity of visitors, but the quality. Sure, go ahead and place a banner ad on the media site if you wish, but there are several reasons you (especially as a *BrandFace*) will want to host and control your own campaign site.

Promotion Potential:

Let's face it, media sales reps are in it to make money. That's their job and I don't blame them. So when they have a chance to control the content, traffic and lead generation, that puts them in the driver's seat. Not only because it means that their website will get additional traffic (so they can sell you more expensive impressions), but they can keep your campaign dollars to themselves. If your content or offer lives on their site, you probably won't be able to advertise the same offer on another media outlet, because a radio station will not promote or send traffic to another media outlet site to fulfill your campaign. However, if you drive prospects directly to a site that you own and control, you can advertise this on any media outlet, anytime, anywhere.

Lead Generation:

On top of the potential promotional dilemma, third party sites will not always hand over the prospect list that is generated from a digital campaign. Meaning, if you have prospects that register to win your prize or sign up to receive or download information you provide, they will have access to the entire list, but will only give you the actual opt-ins from the campaign (those who agreed to be contacted by you). By law, they are correct in doing so, but this means that you can miss out on important information from potential customers, such as the zip codes of those who might be showing the most interest, whether there are more female than male prospects, etc. Even though you may not be able to utilize the email addresses of those who didn't opt in, you can still follow up with direct mail or gain valuable research from the project. If you're paying for a campaign, take control of the final destination.

Tracking:
The ability to track campaign traffic can be very important. While media outlets will provide tracking numbers in terms of how many people clicked on your ad, you definitely want access to the most important numbers, and that's what happens after the ad was clicked. You'll want to know the time spent on your site, whether they viewed your video, which pages were of greatest interest, how many filled out a registration form, etc. The third party site may provide you with tracking reports for a campaign site that lives within their pages, but they will rarely give you inside access to look at the traffic numbers more closely. Conversely, if you set up a free Google Analytics account for your own campaign site, you have full access to break down those analytics any way you want.

EXAMPLES & IDEAS
Product Sales:
Blendtec is a company that makes restaurant quality blenders. The marketing challenge was that their product was seen as 'just another industrial blender', and on top of that, it was priced higher than competing blenders. Their one point of differentiation was the fact that their blenders were tough, virtually indestructible. To prove that point, they shot a series of videos titled 'Will It Blend?' which featured a man in a white lab coat (their face of the brand) attempting to blend various unconventional items in a Blendtec blender. The point was to prove that the item would actually blend without damaging the motor. They posted these videos on the campaign site WillItBlend.com. Even though their main site, Blendtec.com, features all the information about their blenders, the campaign site allows them to promote this specific creative and catchy point of differentiation in a memorable way.

Event:
Michael Kors is one of my favorite designers, and when they launched this campaign I thought it was a brilliant way to enhance their brand and make it relevant to today's young designers and fashion lovers. The campaign site went live early in anticipation of their Fall 2014 runway show in order to educate visitors about the upcoming event. The morning of the fashion show, the site will stream video from the live event, giving visitors a front row

102

view of the fashion show. In addition, on the right hand side of the page they have embedded their Twitter stream, allowing visitors to interact with the brand and with other fans during the event using #allaccesskors.

Contest:

Contests are one of the best ways to capture contact information and build a database. One of my favorites was Olive Garden's sweepstakes contest for a trip to their Culinary Institute of Tuscany. It's not only a fantastic prize, it brings you right to their cooking school, which is the perfect opportunity to demonstrate their culture and connect intimately to the brand. In effect, this trip builds strong brand ambassadors! It's one great way to take their expertise and passion for Italian food and make it the center of their campaign.

Social Media Hub:

A political figure is perhaps one of the best examples of a BrandFace. When Ohio Congressman Pat Tiberi was running for re-election in 2010, we had the opportunity to build a campaign site which would help to educate voters about Pat's insight on important issues. He was regularly posting on several social media platforms as well as utilizing advertorials (paid print ads that appear like articles or editorials) to support his re-election campaign. Our idea was to build an aggregate campaign site which fed all those resources into one place. That strategy allowed him to *promote* just one site, but expose potential voters to all his communication and interaction. We included buttons which allowed voters to donate, volunteer and even request his yard signs. Finally, there was a place for visitors to request specific topics for his next newspaper article. We used the domain name TalkWithPat.com.

_____   **Ron's Message**   _____

Campaign sites are part of the content and search engine optimization process, but they're also excellent for our customers. When we can include everything about a specific concern or product in one place, customers find that easy and convenient.

For example, we have one campaign site which features all of our current special offers. When it comes to our existing customer base, they already know and trust us, so we can occasionally bypass the usual 'get to know us' content and focus on the main goal of continuing to introduce them to new products and services. We segment them on our email marketing list and then we can link directly to this special offers page so they can see products and services they may not yet have. When they reach this page, they see only these featured specials, and at a glance can see what they might see a product or service they need right now.

For instance, an impending storm may make them think about the potential for water in their basement or the need for a generator. By putting these specials in one place, it serves as a reminder and increases the chance that we might have instant feedback. We're constantly thinking of how we can help our customers *continue* to keep their homes drier, cleaner, healthier, safer, and more energy efficient.

Example L: Current Specials Landing Page

Chapter 20:

DIGITAL MARKETING—
INBOUND OR OUTBOUND?

Since the introduction of the internet, the way we market and advertise has drastically changed. I refer to that shift as Mass Media vs. *Me* Media. If we think about the old consumer path to sales (prior to the internet), marketing messages were 'pushed' out to the masses, and consumers responded by calling the business, visiting the location in person and or in some cases even mailing in a response. Today, they almost always head to a computer, tablet or mobile phone to get more information, narrowing their choices prior to making initial contact. Digital Marketing is the quintessential *'me'* media. It's defined as the promotion of products and services using various digital media such as computers, tablets, mobile phones and gaming systems.

Digital Marketing has had a tremendous impact regarding consumer influence through various types of media, as mentioned in the Introduction chapter. So what does this mean for a *BrandFace*? All of these devices and means of marketing provide excellent opportunities for one-to-one communication across multiple platforms.

Though there are many different digital marketing platforms to consider, some rightfully have their own dedicated chapters in this book (*Social Media, Mobile Marketing, Email Marketing*, etc.), and are explored in greater detail. In this chapter, you'll find information on some of the platforms and examples of digital marketing that are not covered in those specific chapters. To begin, let's look at the two different types of digital marketing: *outbound* marketing and *inbound* marketing.

OUTBOUND MARKETING
Outbound marketing (also referred to as *push marketing*) is when you market a message to consumers who have not asked for it and thus may not have a desire or interest for it. An example of this would include placing display or banner ads on a website or sending unsolicited text messages. This kind of marketing is often seen as intrusive or interruptive. I liken it to traditional media messages. They interrupt your programming or content regardless of whether you like it or ask for it.

INBOUND MARKETING
In contrast, *inbound* marketing (also called *pull marketing*) is sending or posting

messages to people who are actively seeking your specific content online. Examples include permission-based email marketing (when consumers have signed up for your list) or when someone subscribes to your blog feed or YouTube channel. There are many examples of inbound marketing throughout this book, and I strongly believe it is the key to creating the relationships and connections that every *BrandFace* desires.

DISPLAY ADS

Display or banner ads have targeting capabilities that can include geo-targeting (targeting by zip code, city or region), demographic targeting (by age, education, income, etc.), behavioral targeting (by lifestyle or interest), contextual ad placement (placing ads next to relevant content) and re-targeting (ads that follow your visitors once they leave your site and continue to browse the web). If you choose a display ad campaign, the best *BrandFace* strategy is to include your photo and branding images in the display ad and to try to be as targeted as possible with both the placement of your ad *and* your message. This is achieved by focusing your ad message to relate specifically to where the ad will be placed. For instance, if you are promoting a second hand furniture store, you might place your ad on sites where consumers are seeking home decorating ideas, such as HGTV.com. Your messaging might be, *'Are you an HGTV junkie? Get your Fix for Less. Click to see our latest arrivals.'* Then link the ad to a page on your site that displays your recent products and connects directly to the prospect (find more on this in the *Beyond the Click* section of this chapter). Overall, however, I believe there are more efficient ways to spend your money than a *push* marketing display ad campaign. I'm sure by now you've already thought of several more impactful ways to advertise as well.

SEARCH ENGINE MARKETING

Search marketing revenue has grown tremendously in the last few years with no signs of slowing. As a result, many advertisers have re-tooled their marketing efforts to focus entirely on search marketing. While I would not recommend the 'search option' alone versus a more integrated approach, search marketing does bring qualified prospects to the table. People who click on a link within a search engine and visit your site purposefully are actively seeking information about a topic, product, service, etc. This means they are already more pre-qualified than the majority of prospects who are exposed to a *push* marketing campaign.

Search engine marketing is a term that encompasses both organic search engine optimization and paid search options, both of which can be utilized with your *BrandFace* approach. Let's take a closer look at the both options and the most effective use of each.

SEO

Search engine optimization (SEO) is utilizing relevant content, keywords, tags, reputable links and embedded content in your website in order to organically boost the search ranking of your site. The impact of a first page Google search return can mean the difference between the success and failure of a business. Natural or 'organic' search returns are based on a series of mathematical formulas or algorithms that are designed to deliver the most useful, relevant and meaningful content based on a user's search query. So how does all this technical stuff play into a *BrandFace* strategy? Very simple…content! Your blog is the single most important ally in your search campaign. It's where you'll share your expertise, exclusive content and more—full of those keywords and information your prospects are searching. A good friend of mine, Don the Idea Guy (a *BrandFace* himself), will wager a bet with anyone that he can get a brand new site on page one of Google within just a few months without spending a dime. And yes, he's done it…by blogging alone! You'll find more relevant information about this topic in the chapter on Content Marketing.

PPC

Paid search, often called PPC (pay per click) or CPC (cost-per-click) is buying or bidding on specific search terms so that your ad shows up when visitors search the keywords you have identified in your campaign. If the visitor clicks on your ad, you pay the agreed upon rate per click. I believe the organic route is more meaningful over time because the results are generated based on relevant content versus paid advertising, and organic search results are viewed as more trustworthy for that reason. However, paid search still attracts qualified prospects that are typing keywords into a search browser in order to actively seek information about a specific subject.

SEO TIPS

You can find many great tips online for organically boosting your search results, but I've compiled a few here which seem to be the most popular in my own research on the subject.

Specials or Promotions:

People often search online for specials and discounts, so it makes sense that any promotional information shared on your site would rank well. Traffic to this page is a good sign that you have a hot prospect on the line, so keep the offers up to date and give your visitors another reason to choose you over your competitors.

Page Titles:
Also called title tags, a page title is the text you see at the top of a web page in your tab which describes your website. For instance, for my BrandFaceStar.com site, the description in the page title includes my subtitle, "Be the face of your business and a star in your industry".

Text vs. Graphics:
Use graphics and photos which display your *BrandFace* imaging, content and information (such as infographics), but don't embed your text in them. Search engines love text, but they don't detect the text if it is embedded within a graphic.

About Us:
This informative page is frequently viewed on a company website, so make sure you have one on yours which tells your story and even includes staff photos and bios.

Exclusive Content:
Beating a dead horse? You bet! You'll see this subject over and over throughout this book because it's a vital part of establishing your authority, expertise and credibility. Keep developing exclusive content because it works.

Embedded Content:
Search engines love content embedded from platforms like YouTube, Flickr and Slideshare (to name just a few). They see these as reputable, established sites specifically used to generate and feed content.

Keyword Navigation:
When considering your top navigation tabs or links, use terms that people often search for in your industry. Amazon.com does a great job of this by creating links to all their product categories.

Blog:
This one should probably be combined with content, because a blog should be your primary content channel when it comes to search. Make your blog a page within your main website for maximum search results.

Inbound Links:
Links from other relevant, reputable sites (especially those with lots of traffic) are an important part of the organic search algorithm. This all ties back to relevant content (again) which others deem worthy enough to link to, thus giving your site and content more credibility. Remember to use keywords that your prospects may use when searching for information. If Google sees

a keyword in a link, it assumes that the page contains content that's relevant to that keyword. Finally, encourage others to link to a specific content page within your site instead of just linking to your home page. Help them get right to the relevant content.

Google Authorship:
Google has an ongoing initiative designed to attribute content to its original author. As a *BrandFace* who provides exclusive content, if you follow the steps to establish authorship, your photo and content headline will show up prominently on your Google search returns. You can establish Google Authorship by connecting your Google+ profile to your original content. So if you haven't yet completed your Google+ profile, do so now, then follow the steps to establish authorship. Instructions can be found at plus.google.com/authorship.

Social Media Feed:
Embedding social media widgets or feeds into your site can be very beneficial. Encourage likes and shares by adding social media 'sharing' widgets next to your content. That makes it easier for your visitors to share your *BrandFace* expertise!

Tag Photos and Videos:
Search engines may not recognize text embedded in an image or graphic, but they do pay attention to tagging. Make sure each photo or video on your site is properly titled according to its content so they index well on the search engines as well.

Internal Hyperlinks:
Utilizing hyperlinks within your site (which link to other helpful content sources on your site) tells search engines that the information is important. For instance, if you have an automotive website and you'd like to share with your new customers the various ways to establish credit (so they can finance a car through your dealership), you might create content on the top ways to achieve that goal. When you consider other pages on your site where this information might be valuable to your visitors, such as the financing and application pages, you can create hyperlinks on those pages to the information on establishing credit.

BEYOND THE CLICK

As mentioned early in this chapter, there are so many different digital marketing platforms, from social to mobile to email, but one follow-through strategy should apply to any of these. In fact, I dedicate an entire training program on this subject when I consult media outlets. That's because many display advertising and search marketing campaigns frankly do it wrong.

It matters what's on the other side of the click. Unfortunately, many paid display or search ads link to the home page of a company's website, and that is rarely where the important information lives. Don't make your prospects think. They clicked on an ad because they were interested in the message. That's the first hurdle! So make it easy for them and take them directly to the information they seek. Second, it's on your dime, so you want to make certain that the exact message you want them to receive—and action you want them to take—is apparent right away. You can achieve that with a campaign page that lives on your main site which has this specific information or through a dedicated campaign site or landing page with a marketable URL. Determine your campaign goals in advance. Whether you want prospects to view a video about your new product, download your 'Top 10 Tips', register to win a contest or purchase your new book, make your time and money work for you by getting them right to the task at hand. You can learn a lot more about this in the chapter on Campaign Sites.

Ron's Message

We know that most people do homework online today before making a purchase, large or small. And it's our job to make sure that we're not only the prevalent choice, but that we stand out above all others in our image and messaging.

We've run display ads on various local media websites, Google Ad campaigns and retargeting campaigns on a network of websites. Just as we do with all other ads, we include my image in all our creative digital marketing. The thing I appreciate most about digital marketing is the ability to immediately connect to specific content our customer is seeking. For instance, if they click on an ad about sump pumps, they might land on a promotional sales opportunity and educational information about the pumps. On that page, we also have the opportunity to link out to our customer testimonials, social media platforms and more. It's a continual opportunity for our customers to learn more while in front of their computer or portable device.

Example M: Basement Doctor Banner Ad

Chapter 21:

NON TRADITIONAL ADVERTISING
IDEAS THAT ROCK

This category encompasses many different types of advertising, but is generally defined as anything outside of the usual print, radio, television, direct mail, billboards and collateral materials. Instead of defining each here, I've decided to give examples of the effective use of various types of non-traditional advertising.

Sports Arenas:
Whether professional, college or local school level, on-site signage offers excellent opportunities to present yourself and your brand to a loyal, recurring audience with frequency. Local school sponsorships are looked upon with great favor and patrons often reward those advertisers for supporting their local teams. One example of execution might be a local mobile phone company or internet provider partnering with an anti-bullying non-profit. Signage at a local high school football field could say something like, "TAKE MY MONEY! We'll donate $100 to *End Cyber Bullying* every time the Tigers score a touchdown." What a great way to show your support to the school or charity and achieve recognition as a community leader regarding the bullying challenges that plague all our schools.

Busses:
Imagine your image on the side of a city bus! It's a dream fulfilled by many a *BrandFace*. One great example sparked my interest when I first moved to Columbus, Ohio. Bob Juniper owns Three-C Body Shop, an auto and collision repair company. His strategy positions Three-C as Central Ohio's *Direct Repair Alternative* versus the 'Preferred Shop Programs' that allow insurers to control your auto repair. Bob believes that preferred shops are really only preferred by insurance companies. His creative take on this message has been seen on busses throughout Central Ohio.

Benches:
I'm sure you've seen benches with 'See, you looked!' or 'Advertise here!' signs. There are several ways to get super creative with bench advertising, but perhaps the most recognizable would be a bold color or shape that coincides with your business colors and strategy. Pink benches for breast cancer awareness or back bench slats shaped like oars for a boating company are just two examples. Always put your image on the bench signage!

Vehicles:
Unusual vehicles definitely make a splash and capture attention wherever they go. Take the Oscar Meyer Weinermobile (shaped like a hot dog on a bun), perhaps the most recognizable promotional vehicle in America (besides the Batmobile!). Since its debut, others have surfaced, including vehicles shaped like ice cream cones, cupcakes, eggs and insects!

Shopping Baskets:
One of the campaigns that struck me most was executed in grocery stores on behalf of the non-profit *Feed South Africa*. They placed large photo decals in the bottom of a shopping cart that featured a starving child looking up and holding out his hands, as though begging for food. It captured my heart right away. Who would *not* give to this campaign? It's a powerful demonstration of using the recipient of the donations as the face of the brand (the starving child) and in the location where we all purchase food. Hats off to such a creative and meaningful connection.

Paper Goods:
My real estate client had a phenomenal idea to brand his business by providing paper plates, cups and napkins to local schools, churches and organizations for their events. It's a small price to pay to have your logo and tagline literally in the hands of so many prospects. I absolutely love this idea, and we're in the process now of creating these products for him. Sometimes it's the small things that make the biggest impact.

Billboards:
While billboards have been around forever and are not really considered non-traditional, I just had to throw this one in here. I was visiting a client in the Atlanta area when I passed a billboard along I-85 featuring a bald man with the message, "Injured? Don't pull your hair out! MyBaldLawyer.com". Genius! I loved the approach and his strategy, which is to eradicate the stereotype that most lawyers are uptight and unapproachable. Chandler Mason (Mason & Associates) uses this humorous concept to do just that!

Creative Signage:
Poole's BBQ, a restaurant in Elijay, Georgia, was informed that they couldn't put up roadside signage to promote their business, so they cleverly began selling small wooden pigs to patrons and fans, who promptly covered an entire hillside near the restaurant. It's known as the Pig Hill of Fame. "In January 1992, the Associated Press asked Oscar Poole about the 307 pigs on the hill at that time (there are now over 3000!). Four days later, the AP ran the story in over 1000 newspapers. Since then, the Pig Hill of Fame has become a

legend and a North Georgia landmark." (Source: PoolesBarBQ.com) Talk about a non-traditional approach to some great signage *and* PR opportunities for the owner!

Ron's Message

I'd like to think we've been pioneers when it comes to non-traditional advertising. We've pretty much tried it all! For several years we've placed large American flags all around our office for the 4th of July. We're on a very busy corner lot, so it gets a lot of attention. We've advertised on billboards, both traditional and digital. We have also advertised on t-shirts, during local sports programs and at concert venues.

Another non-traditional way we advertise is simple, but very effective. Our trucks are wrapped with our logo and services, so everyone knows when and where the Basement Doctor is 'on the job'. One of our promotional vehicles is actually an ambulance, which ties in nicely with the Basement Doctor brand!

Example N: Ambulance Wrapped As Promotional Vehicle

EXAMPLE IMAGES

Below is a QR (quick response) code which links to a full color *BrandFace* portfolio of all the items on the next several pages. If you've never used a QR code before, here is some information which will guide you through the process.

Your smart phone must be web enabled. You will need a QR reader app to use these codes. Most QR readers are free. Simply go to the marketplace area on your smart phone (the place where you download apps) and search for 'QR reader'.

Once the QR reader application is downloaded, open the app on your phone and hold your phone up to the code, positioning the code within the guidelines shown on your phone so your phone can scan the code. When the code is successfully scanned, the QR reader on your phone will link you directly to the portfolio.

(www.brandfacestar.com/homeimprovementexamples)

Example A: The Basement Doctor Jingle
(www.brandfacestar.com/bdjingle)

Example B: Sample photo shoot images

Example C: The Basement Doctor website

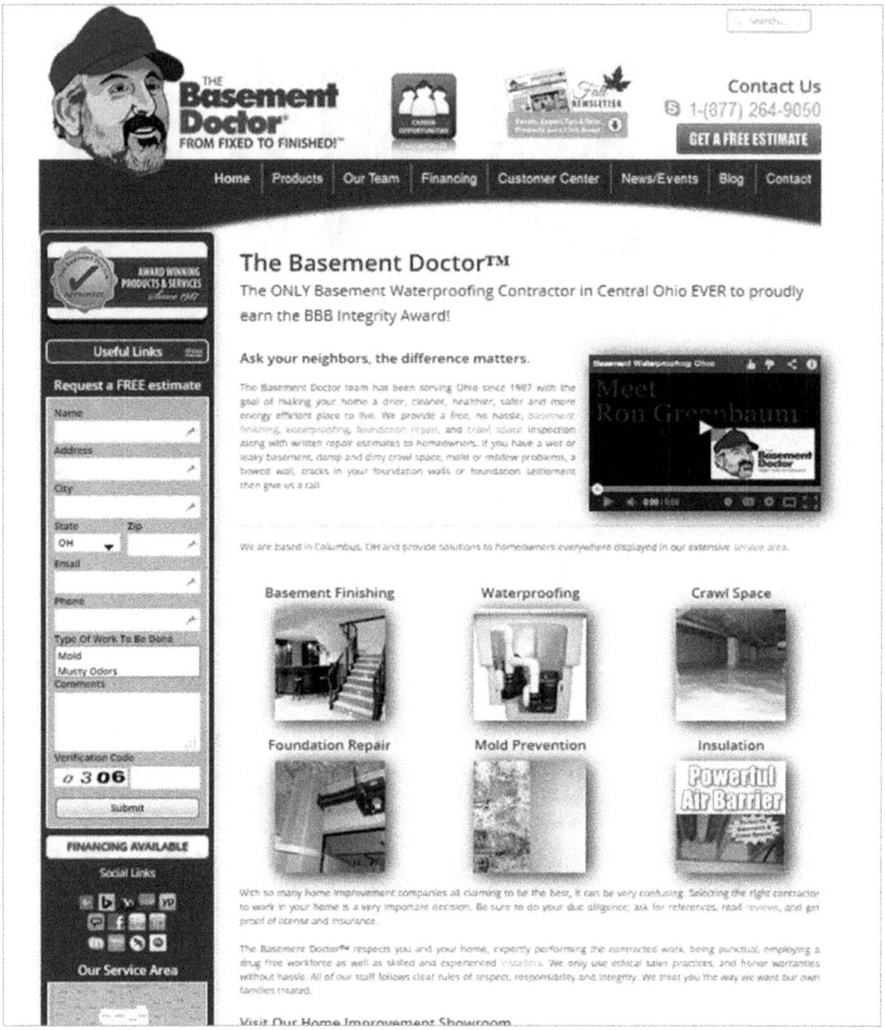

Example D: 'Bowed or Cracked' educational video
(www.brandfacestar.com/bowedorcrackedvideo)

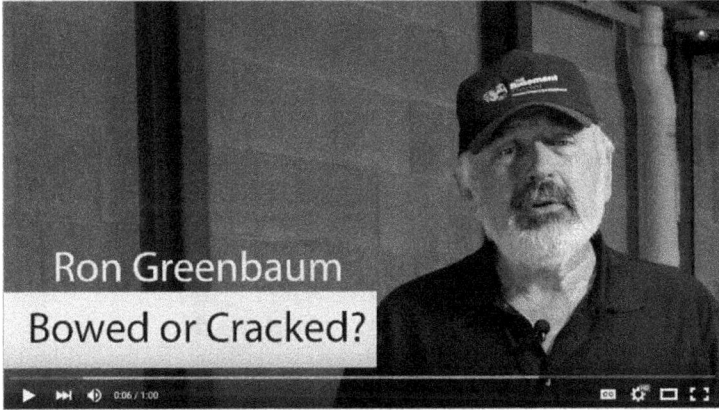

Ron Greenbaum
Bowed or Cracked?

Example E: Ron's personal business card

Ron Greenbaum
Principal
Office: 1-877-DRY-TIME (379-8463)
Cell: (614) 206-4752
RGreenbaum@MyBasementDoctor.com

- Basement Waterproofing
- Foundation Repair
- Crawl Space Solutions
- Mold Prevention
- Basement Finishing

MyBasementDoctor.com · BasementFinishingOhio.com

Example F: Consumer's Guide brochure

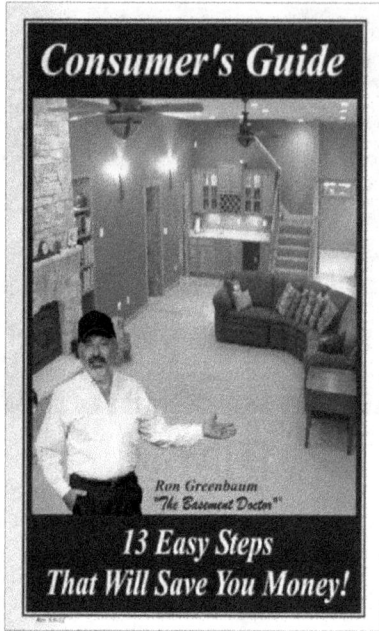

Example G: Spring Newsletter

THE **Basement Doctor®**
FROM FIXED TO FINISHED!™

See Back for our 2015 *Spring Special*

HOUSE CALLS

www.MyBasementDoctor.com • 614-372-6813

Spring 2015

Is your home ready for *Spring?*

Take action to prevent flooding with 6 easy tips

By Ron Greenbaum,
The Basement Doctor

(5)

UNDERSTAND YOUR INSURANCE POLICY

Carefully check your policy to see if common plumbing leaks are covered. Additional coverage may be required.

EXTERIOR MAINTENANCE **(1)**

Clear gutters of all debris, extend downspout lines away from the foundation, and regrade the soil away from the home.

(4)

FREE YOUR HOME FROM LEFTOVER ICE & SNOW

Snow can melt and then refreeze in foundation cracks for long periods of time.

(2)

STOP RAIN FROM ENTERING THROUGH BASEMENT WINDOWS

If you have below-grade basement windows, window well covers are an effective solution to preventing rain water from coming into your home.

(3)

MAINTAIN YOUR SUMP PUMP SYSTEM

If you have a sump pump in your basement, make sure it is plugged in and working properly. It is important to clean your system each spring before the heavy rains begin.

(6)

KNOW WHO TO CALL

Find a reputable contractor who offers emergency services so that your house is a priority if flooded.

What's INSIDE?

PAGE **2**	PAGE **3**	PAGE **4**
Turn Your House Upside Down On the Job Case Study	The Basement Doctor Gives Back	Spring Special! Annual Maintenance Service

Example H: Fall Newsletter

120

Example I: 'Meet Ron Greenbaum' video
(www.brandfacestar.com/meetronvideo)

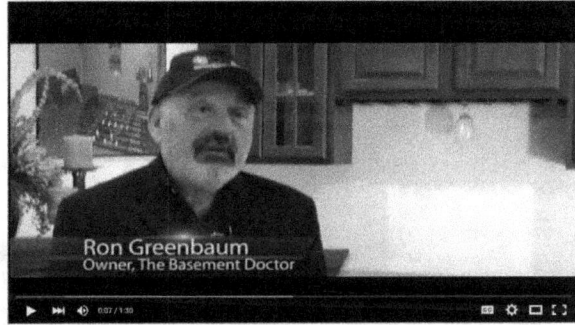

Example J: Ron's Bloopers video
(www.brandfacestar.com/ronbloopervideo)

The Basement Doctor's Bloopers & Gag Reel from Columbus Ohio

Example K: 'All Sum Pumps Fail' radio commercial
(www.brandfacestar.com/sumppumpradio)

Example L: Current Specials Campaign Site

Example M: Basement Doctor Banner Ad

Example N: Ambulance Wrapped As Promotional Vehicle

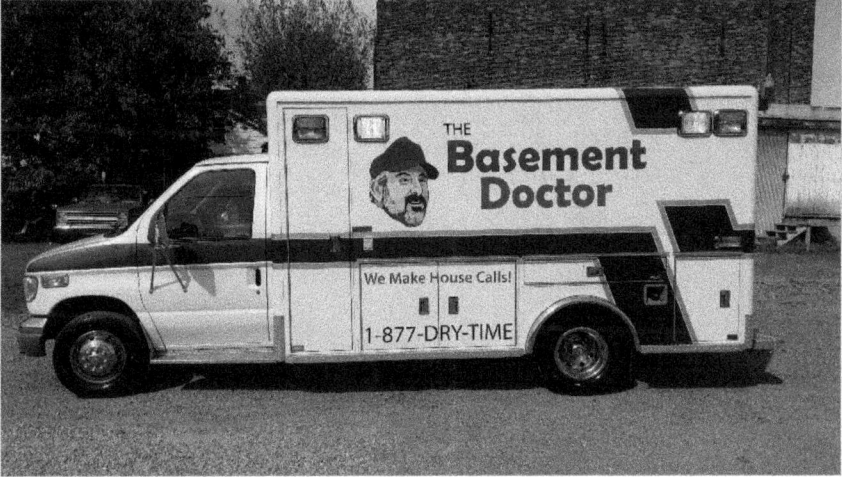

Example O: Ron Making a Donation to Maria's Message

Example P: Flyer for Charity Event

Example Q: Basement Doctor Billboard

Example R: 'House Calls' eNewsletter

The Basement Doctor
FROM FIXED TO FINISHED!

House Calls

SCHEDULE AN APPOINTMENT
(888) 494-9344

CONNECT WITH US

Waterproofing | Crawl Space | Foundation Repair | Basement Finishing | Energy Saving Products

Get Your Home *Winter-Ready!*

Taking a few steps now will keep you safe and warm all season long.

Winter weather brings chilly temperatures and high utility bills, but The Basement Doctor can help keep money in your pockets, and make sure the cold air stays outside where it belongs. Here are some simple fixes that will pay off big this season.

1. Make sure your attic has the proper amount of insulation.

2. Seal leaks and cracks, especially around windows, doors, electrical outlets and pipes to save money and get rid of drafts.

3. Clear gutters to protect against ice damming.

4. Properly insulate your crawl space with a Radiant Barrier.

See Ron with Karina Nova of 10TV. He gave advice on how to prevent costly winter damage!

Example S: 'Thank You' email response

YOU *matter to* US.

From Ron Greenbaum,
The Basement Doctor

Thank you for choosing The Basement Doctor!

We understand that you had a lot of options when it came to selecting a home improvement contractor. We of course strive to be the best. But in today's world, it is difficult to set yourself apart from other companies on the internet. That is why we depend on our customers to be our trusted voice.

Our team members participate in ongoing training to ensure that they have provided you with the highest level of service possible. If you feel that our team has met or exceeded your expectations, would you please take a few minutes out of your day to write them a review?

Was there something that a Project Manager or Foreman did that really wowed you? Were they punctual and polite? Did they respect your property and clean up after the job was complete?

These are goals that we set for our crews. We hope these goals were met during your project, and that we earned a 5-Star review from you. You can post your review online by clicking on the icons below. We thank you in advance for your honest feedback.

f	g+	BBB	yp
CLICK HERE to review us on FACEBOOK!	**CLICK HERE** to leave a Google+ REVIEW!	**CLICK HERE** to submit a BBB REVIEW!	**CLICK HERE** to review us on YELLOW PAGES!

These links are to trusted third-party sites. They will require an account to post your review. If you would like to submit a review without a login and password, you can do so directly on <u>our website</u>.

Example T: Basement Doctor Facebook Page

CONSUMERS CHOICE AWARD 2014 — Waterproofing
CONSUMERS CHOICE AWARD 2014 — Finishing
CONSUMERS CHOICE AWARD 2014 — Foundation
TOP WORK PLACES 2015
CEO 10

Award-Winning Products and Services Since 1987

Basement Waterproofing · Foundation Repair · Finishing
Crawl Space Solutions · Mold Prevention / Removal

Basement Doctor FROM FIXED TO FINISHED

For a Drier, Cleaner, Healthier, Safer, More Energy Efficient Hom

Call me now! (614) 682-836

The Basement Doctor
Contractor · Home

Contact Us ▾   👍 Liked ▾   ➤ Share   ...

Timeline   About   Services   Reviews   More ▾

2,583 likes · 3 this week
Jodi Kotzin Thomas and 15 other friends

89 were here · this week
Ana Valdivia and 3 others

View Pages Feed
See posts from other Pages

Invite friends to like this Page

2,298 post reach this week

Let People Find The Basement Doctor

📝 Status   🖼 Photo / Video   🎁 Offer, Event +

Write something...

The Basement Doctor
Published by Ron Lyles [?] · 1 hr · 🌐

Don't let freezing temperatures catch you with your guard down!

In bitterly cold temperatures, your pipes are vulnerable to freezing. When your pipes freeze, your sump pump can back up sending water back into your home! Our simple solution is Freeze Relief! Call today to set up your

Example U: WhiteCap Direct Mail Postcard (front & back)

Chapter 22:

INCORPORATING PHILANTHROPY
IN YOUR IMAGE

One of the simplest definitions of philanthropy comes from the Merriam-Webster dictionary: "The practice of giving money and time to help make life better for other people". It is this spirit of giving back that is the backbone of successful businesses. To whom much is given, much is required.
I wrote this book to help you achieve success both in recognition and revenue. And I strongly believe that giving back sets the tone and the course for both. I am a proponent of the *Law of Attraction*, which states that focusing on positive thoughts can bring about positive results. If thinking alone can result in positivity, imagine what *doing* positive things can mean!

Every successful business owner or leader I've known throughout my lifetime believes in something deeper than profit margins or their face on a billboard. As stated in the dedication portion of this book, there is a story behind every human being, and that deeply personal story is often the guiding force behind their philanthropic efforts.

Whatever your reasons for giving back, *market* it for the right reasons as well. The natural outcome is that it will help your image, your reputation and your business—if only by law of attraction. That said, I wouldn't be doing my job correctly if I didn't tell you to make sure you share information about the organizations or people you support with your public.

One of my clients was super sensitive about this topic. She did not want to discuss and especially publish or broadcast *anything* about her work with charities because she felt it would appear disingenuous. She didn't want the public to think that she was taking advantage of the organizations she supports. She was so steadfast in this belief that I wasn't sure if I was going to break through her resolve.

However, having worked with many charity organizations over the years while serving in a media sales role, I was allowed behind the scenes to witness what charities don't often share with the public. The truth is, charity organizations *want* you to publicize your efforts to assist them. They *count on it* to promote themselves and their mission. They are *thrilled* when they hear that you have hundreds or thousands of followers on Facebook, Twitter or LinkedIn. That could mean more supporters, more ambassadors of their own brand, and ultimately more donations. And frankly, many of these organizations have limited budgets and staff. Their very existence often depends on the generosity and publicity from their supporters. When I explained this to my client, she definitely understood and is now an ardent public supporter of her charities.

The key to tying in charity work as a *BrandFace* is to *make it all about the charity*. Each post, press release or article should be written to highlight the great works of the charity and to extend gratitude for their mission—and to your own staff members who unselfishly give their time or money to support the cause. You should be the bystander, the conduit through which these great works take place.

Most business owners who give back do so strategically, and most will share that the decision regarding which charity organizations to assist can be a tough one. Think about the issues you are most passionate about. The things you care about most will provide the greatest satisfaction to you and the organizations you choose to assist. Here are a few examples of creative ties in giving back across various categories:

IDEAS BY INDUSTRY
Home Improvement:
You and your staff can volunteer for Habitat for Humanity and work on a project together. Promote this in advance on social media and include a pledge button so your followers can donate to the charity to support you and your team. Each team member can have a dedicated donation link and compete to see who raises the most money through social media for the charity.

Automotive:
Consider donating a car to a family in need or partnering with a local charity to promote car donations in lieu of trade-ins when someone purchases a vehicle from you. Instead of a trade-in campaign, call it 'Trade It Forward'.

Coffee Shop:
Offer free coffee to veterans on Veteran's Day or to police officers or members of your local fire house one day each week. You can participate in this initiative even if you don't own the coffee shop! Offer to partner with the coffee shop and purchase the coffee cups specifically used for that purpose. Put a personal message on the cups such as "A small token of our gratitude to thank you for your service" along with your company logo and the logo of the coffee shop.

Carpet Cleaning:

Donate a portion of the sales from your pet stain remover to your local area Humane Society. When your carpet cleaning technicians enter a customer's home (who has a pet), leave behind a pet treat attached to a free sample of stain remover and a postcard promoting animal adoption.

Grocery:

Host a canned goods drive at your store. Get super creative and join forces with a nearby movie theater to host a 'Canned Film Festival' weekend. Each can of food that movie-goers bring will earn them $2.00 off their movie ticket. It's a great way to stock your local food bank and drive traffic to both the grocery store and the movie theatre.

Dry Cleaning:

In almost every market there are clothing drives such as 'Coats for Kids'. Offer to become the drop-off point for those donated coats and jackets, and then clean them for free before distributing to families in need.

Restaurant:

Host a weekend pancake breakfast to support a local charity. As the restaurant owner, you could send personal video messages across social media inviting the public to the event, and another set of videos inviting local business owners to take part in the event by serving as your local celebrity wait staff. It's another *BrandFace* moment for your patrons and your peers, and all proceeds benefit your chosen charity.

Pharmacy:

Host a weekend health fair which includes free testing for things like blood pressure and diabetes. Work with local health care partners to provide the technicians for testing, and promote to each other's networks in advance of the event. It's a great service to those who can't afford to visit a doctor regularly, and a great tie-in for the pharmacy when they do need medication.

Real Estate:

A successful real estate broker or agent knows their community well, so who better to serve as host to your local non-profit organizations? Shoot one video per month from a non-profit location in your community. The video should introduce the non-profit President or Director and share basic information about the organization. Post it on your website under 'Volunteer Opportunities' and be the local hub for residents to learn about places and ways they can give back.

Salon & Spa:
One non-profit organization holds an annual Mother-Daughter Makeover event for family members of those with life-altering illnesses. It gives caretaking family members a break from hospitals, testing and the general stress that can overwhelm a family facing an illness. A local salon dedicates one day per year to provide free services for this event. It's a heartwarming event that improves the lives of all involved.

Ron's Message

I want to leave a legacy of giving back, beyond just a home improvement company in Columbus, Ohio. I want to provide for the people and institutions that need it most. I want to show my appreciation for the great life I've been given and I'd like to think I've done an adequate job so far. I realize that giving back is at the core of what this company is all about.

Over these last thirty years, we've supported so many charity organizations. All the charity events we've taken part in are very special to me, but one in particular stands out. I helped support and launch an event called the Victory Canteen. Throughout this preparation, our internal marketing team began to look like an event promotions company! Victory Canteen is a special dinner and dance to support an organization called Honor Flight Columbus. They celebrate our World War II and Korean War Veterans by flying them to Washington, D.C. to visit memorials dedicated to their important service at no cost to them. It was a magical event, and I was proud to be a part of it.

In 2015, I was named a finalist for the Corporate Caring Award, designed to recognize individuals and companies who consistently give back and are known for their strong involvement in the community. Among all my philanthropic contributions, it's truly an honor to be recognized for this award.

As I write this, I'm participating in an event called Beards for the Boys, a fundraiser to fight prostate and testicular cancer and fund research. If we raise $50,000, I have agreed to shave my iconic beard!

Example O: Ron Supporting 'Maria's Message'
Example P: Promotional Flyer for Charity Contest

Chapter 23:

PUBLIC RELATIONS—

ARE YOU NEWSWORTHY?

According to the Public Relations Society of America, "Public relations is a strategic communication process that builds mutually beneficial relationships between organizations and their publics." (PRSA.org, March 2014). I believe the key to this definition lies in the words 'mutually beneficial'.

News coverage by a reputable publication or source is arguably the best way to establish credibility. It means someone else has taken notice of your work, and considers it worthy of publishing or broadcasting due to your expertise or insight on the matter. And consumers notice because it's non-biased and clearly not paid advertising.

In order to determine whether you should submit a story for consideration, first, you need to decide whether the information you are putting forth is newsworthy. Here are some questions to help you make that determination.

IS IT NEWSWORTHY?
Do you have a very unique product or service that no one else has?
Is your own background unique or interesting? (BrandFace candidates have a unique story)
Is there a message that is topical for the times? (Think gluten-free, organic, recycling, etc.)
Does your product, service or idea improve the lives of others in some unique way?
Do you have a compelling story or customer testimonial to share about it?
Is there a unique benefit to a specific category?
Is there a specific focus on a category? (Pets, teenagers, social media, etc.)
Is there a philanthropic focus?
Is there an educational angle to exploit?
Is there a local or regional angle on a trending news story?

ADVANCED PREPARATION
I'm a big believer in the saying that 'luck is what happens when preparation meets opportunity'. That definitely applies to public relations. Here are some suggestions to get you prepared to jump in quickly and shine brightly when the opportunities for media coverage come knocking. Note that most of these items are explained in greater detail in the Content Marketing chapter.

Publish:
One of the quickest ways to establish expertise in your industry is to publish

your works. Consider e-books, white papers, articles and traditional books. One of my favorite publications was written by one of my clients, Ron Greenbaum, The Basement Doctor. Ron owns the number one basement and foundation repair company in his market. I was reviewing his YouTube video collection one day when I came across a speech he delivered at Columbus State Community College in 2009. He was invited as the keynote speaker to address their Leadership Council. His speech focused on the 'things he believed' about running a business, hiring employees and other beliefs which earned his company number one status in his industry. I boldly informed Ron that this speech would be turned into a book one day. After persistent nagging (which he is grateful for today!), we worked together to produce a promotional mini-book called "The Basement Doctor from the Ground Up…25 Things I Believe". The 25 topics were also timely, as they coincided with his company's 25th anniversary. In February of 2014, that book was published. It's a fantastic marketing tool to distribute at his events and appearances, and serves as an excellent example of expertise and authority.

News or Media Page:
Add a News or Media page to your website. It makes the search for pertinent information much simpler. On this page, you'll include things like a downloadable press kit, TV interviews, press releases, news articles and any other related information.

Blog:
Blogging is critical for several reasons, but establishing expertise is at the top of the list. In addition to writing for the education of your prospects, consider what news organizations may be looking for as well. Headlines are very important! Include keywords in your headlines that are relevant to your industry and especially to specific challenges or topics that are currently trending.

Interview Others in Industry:
A very effective way to establish expertise is by interviewing others in your industry, preferably those who are seeking the same customer type. Find someone who has expertise in another subset of your industry. For instance, if you're a coffee shop owner who regularly blogs about different coffee types and flavors, you might consider interviewing someone who has traveled overseas to learn how the finest coffee beans are harvested. Before you conduct the interview, request that they, too, post the interview on their website, blog, e-newsletter, social media channels, etc. This produces a win-win scenario and can expose each of you to a wider audience.

Press Release:

Write press releases for every newsworthy occasion within your company. When you add a new product or service that is unique or exclusive, when you or one of your employees receives an award or when you host an event or participate in a local charity event. Post your press release on your website and blog. A great resource for distributing your press release to media outlets is PressReleaseSender.com. It's a paid, but reasonably priced, option. You'll find options which range from simply reviewing and distributing your press release (with a guarantee that over 100 media sites will publish it) to setting up an interview with you, writing your press release for you and then distributing it on your behalf.

Advertise:

You may be thinking that this category doesn't belong here, and you *should* be right. However, as someone with years of experience working with media outlets, I can tell you that there are times when an advertiser will take priority over a non-advertiser for a news story. If you are spending money with a media outlet, try to leverage that (in a subtle way). Don't assume that your story should take precedent. Simply send your communication through appropriate channels, but make sure to copy your sales representative or at least let them know you have submitted newsworthy information for review. If you approach with courtesy and humility, your chances are good. Contact the News Director at the media outlet and try this approach: "I have attached some information on a unique story about (insert subject matter) that I thought you might consider newsworthy. I realize this is completely separate from my advertising agreement with you, and that it may not receive coverage. But please take a look and let me know if it's of interest to you. If so, I will make myself available at your convenience for further discussion."

Follow Journalists & Reporters:

Most journalists and reporters have LinkedIn pages and Twitter accounts, so connecting and following on those platforms can help you learn a great deal about them. You may be able to learn about each individual's focus, so when it's time to reach out to them about a specific subject, you've done your homework. One organization which can help you connect with experienced reporters is called Help A Reporter Out (HARO). This website, HelpaReporterOut.com, connects reporters with expert sources in order to help them feed great content to media outlets. Become a member and offer to provide articles and information in your area of expertise. The site sends you daily notifications of any news story opportunities in the subject matters you have chosen so you have an opportunity to submit an article for possible publication.

Follow Relevant Blogs:
Just as interviewing others in your industry can help you widen your own network, the same is true when you follow relevant blogs. Similar people travel in similar circles. Make sure to comment occasionally on their posts. That earns credibility and can expose your thought process to their network.

Local Media Relationships:
Connect with local media news directors, who often make the decision regarding broadcasting or publishing a story. Follow them on social channels and send them helpful information on occasion. Be careful about communicating too often, and when you do, make sure it's timely and relevant.

Identify Media Opportunities:
Stay informed about your industry. If you're a landscape nursery, find out when the local home and garden shows take place. Learn when newspapers plan to print their special sections, which generally focus on seasonal topics or local events. Offer to do an interview or submit an article on the topic surrounding the upcoming section or event. If you're a roofing company, pay close attention to the weather and offer your advice and tips to homeowners prior to an impending windstorm or other inclement weather.

Give Back:
Your work with local charities will carry more weight as a *BrandFace*, a known entity. Think about the issues you are most passionate about. Is it pet welfare, child abuse, domestic abuse, poverty, a specific type of cancer, our armed services, etc.? When submitting story ideas to the press, make sure the focus is on the charity. You'll find more details about this in the chapter on Philanthropy.

Win Awards:
Any award your company earns is worthy of a press release. In your release, tie it back to your community, and show gratitude to those inside and outside your organization that may be responsible for the award. This shows humility and willingness to allow your own staff or customers to shine.

Develop a Press Kit:
Sometimes a great press kit can mean the difference in getting your story published or shared. When news organizations are seeking information, a professional representation along with your accomplishments and background information makes their decision easier to justify, and your competitors will pale in comparison. You'll find details regarding your press

kit in the About You chapter.

--------------- **Ron's Message** ---------------

The best advertising is the type you can't purchase. I've been asked to appear numerous times on local TV news programs to address basement topics. And each time I appear, our business has increased as a direct result. If you have integrity about what you do and you do it for the right reasons (and with consistency), you will become the authority that is synonymous with a *BrandFace* approach.

I've been a guest on radio shows and a contributing author for Waterproof Magazine. I've been fortunate to have dozens of articles written about me over the years. I've been the recipient of the Consumer's Choice Award (multiple years), a Small Business of the Year Award, Better Business Bureau Torch Award Winner, Angie's List Super Service Award Winner, CEO Magazine's '15 Business Superstars', and Smart CEO's 'Top 100 Best Run Companies' Winner. These are the titles that you can't buy, and the ones that will provide the most credibility in the marketplace. A strong brand can command a premium price.

Chapter 24:

USING TRADITIONAL MEDIA
IN A DIGITAL WORLD

Traditional media has drastically changed over the last couple of decades. As I'll outline in the pages ahead, each of the big three (newspaper, television, radio) has been impacted by the introduction of numerous competitors, which have splintered their respective audiences. I believe the most important role that traditional media plays now is the ability to drive a loosely targeted (by today's standards) group of people online to connect on a more one-to-one level with a brand. Connection or engagement depends on your campaign goals, but can include educating the prospect about a product, service, event, promotion or initiative, capturing contact information for one-to-one communication or building social media fans and followers, to name a few goals.

Let's take a moment to look at the shift that has taken place with regard to traditional media. I call this shift 'mass media to *me* media'. Before the introduction of the internet, our advertising choices were limited, at least compared to today's options. Advertisers mostly used television, radio and print to push a message to a larger group of consumers. They had limited print space and commercial time to tell their prospects who they were, why someone should do business with them, what made them different, what their special offer might be and where to find them. The consumer response usually fell into two categories—call the business for more information or visit the business location. Sounds pretty simple, right?

Then along comes the digital realm, which completely removes the limitations inherent in traditional media. Not only does the internet provide unlimited space and engagement options, it has proven over time to be the most personal medium of all. You can view a video, read a story, listen to music, find your favorite restaurant location, look at photos, seek opinions and much more. Additionally, the targeting capabilities are tremendous. We can determine a person's age, occupation, interests, recent purchases, shopping habits, banking preferences, viewing habits and more just by following their movement online and capturing their information as they enter it. You can imagine the upheaval this has created among traditional media purists.

In response to this upheaval, in 2007 we launched Remerge, a consulting firm with the sole purpose of helping traditional media understand, integrate and make money by combining traditional and digital media offerings for their advertisers. I found traditional media's initial response to the internet fascinating. Owners and managers were complaining that they were losing advertising dollars to digital. Their mindset was that the internet was another competitor, which perplexed me. Much of our early success in consulting was due to the fact that we were able to convince media outlets that the internet was not a competitor, but an *ally*. After all, no one owns the internet (not even Al Gore)! It's a level playing field, and the internet should be considered a partner, not a competitor. Our advice to traditional media was to use the internet to extend their own media brands and to use the strength of their reach to lead their audience online in order to connect their advertisers with prospects and eventually help to turn those prospects into customers. We argued that yes, traditional media was losing advertising dollars to digital, but that didn't mean those dollars had to belong to someone else. It was up to each traditional media outlet to provide ideas and solutions which integrated their existing product with digital offerings.

Apart from a sales perspective, traditional media has since seen massive audience shifts as well. The larger audiences they were once known for have fallen victim to fragmentation due to ever-growing digital options. All of these things are leaving media outlets with tough choices and advertisers with lackluster returns.

So, after this tirade, do I think that traditional media is dead? Absolutely not. Perhaps 'dead as we once knew it' might apply. Even though big shifts have taken place and media outlets are continuing to evolve toward more online or mobile options, the respective audiences are still intact, just to a smaller degree. I look at every advertising opportunity as case by case. A great idea can produce excellent results if executed properly, regardless of the platform and audience size. You just need to make sure the price you pay is relative to your expected return on investment.

Now that I've set the stage for the broader picture, let's break down the big three (TV, radio and newspaper) and discuss how a *BrandFace* can utilize each to leverage their reach, targeting capabilities and exclusive content opportunities.

RADIO
As you may have guessed, I'm a big fan of terrestrial radio. It was the catalyst for my *BrandFace* fever. Of the big three, radio has always been a more personal, immediate communication vehicle. It's in our cars, often impacting us with an important message just prior to the point of purchase or while we are in a position to react quickly. The ability to target by our music choice,

belief system and lifestyle is powerful. This medium, though, has been greatly affected by several things. First, the monopolizing ownership groups have changed what made radio popular, which is personality and locality. The larger operations are regionalizing staffs and even using air talent across multiple markets to save money. Local morning shows have been replaced with slick-sounding syndicated teams who laugh a lot, but never mention your local stories, streets or points of interest. A lot has changed, for sure, including the introduction of direct competitors. However, given all these changes, radio still commands large audiences and is still a powerful, personal medium for a *BrandFace*. Let's look at some tips for utilizing this popular medium.

RADIO TIPS
Frequency:
When considering a radio schedule, remember that people are bombarded with thousands of advertising messages daily. You need two things to stand out: you must have a different and compelling message and the audience must hear it enough times to be motivated to take action. At best, there are only a certain percentage of people in the market for what you're promoting at any given time, no matter the product or service. Work with your sales representative to make sure your messages reaches people enough times to make an impact.

Placement:
If you can't afford to advertise on radio seven days a week, choose a window of time (one or two days or day parts) and focus all your ads within that time frame. No, you will not reach 100% of that station's audience, but you will reach a smaller percentage enough times to make an impact. Don't water down your advertising schedule. I've witnessed at least half a dozen success stories from advertisers who launched their careers by starting with overnight spots only. Every platform, every time, has an audience. The secret to success lies in how you use it and how much you pay for it.

Programming:
Whenever you have an opportunity to embed yourself into the programming, you stand out. Think about the fact that most commercial breaks contain anywhere from six to ten commercials on average. Obviously, some listeners tend to tune out or switch the station during these long breaks, which means they may miss your ad altogether. If you purchase a weather or news sponsorship though, your business usually gets mentioned just before and after the report, a time frame when most listeners are actively listening, or at least aren't switching the station. It's also common today for local AM stations to sell blocks of programming to local advertisers who want to

produce and air their own show. For instance, a home improvement company can have a half hour show that consists of home improvement tips and discussion, along with live calls from listeners. It's an excellent way for a *BrandFace* to demonstrate expertise. I recall a successful local weekend jazz show produced by Andy Geiger, who at the time was the Athletic Director at the Ohio State University. Andy's hobby and passion was jazz music, so he created and produced his own jazz show in Columbus, Ohio. The show was called *Classic Jazz Masters by Andy Geiger*. His high profile position at OSU made him recognizable in the community, and his involvement with the jazz show added another dimension to his *BrandFace* status.

Interviews:
As part of a public relations strategy or negotiated with your ad schedule, on-air interviews provide a credible and personal platform to share your expertise. Keep in mind that these interviews might not always happen on the morning shows. Ask each radio station about interview opportunities in other programming segments. For example, one station I worked with aired a public service show each Sunday morning, which included local community topics such as economic development, non-profit initiatives, newsworthy events and more. I was able to secure interviews for my clients within that show quite often. While the audience count was generally lower than other times of the week, we leveraged that content by posting it on their websites or social media platforms.

Endorsements:
Endorsements have been used successfully on all platforms, but I chose to include it in this section because as a *BrandFace*, you may be wondering why you should even consider using any type of endorser when you are the face of the brand. Generally, you don't need it. However, I wouldn't rule it out. I just have one simple guideline. Always appear alongside the endorser! Never lose your *BrandFace* opportunity, but enhance it with another credible figure-head who can strengthen your message. Also, use endorsers strategically and for finite time frames. *You* should remain the most recognizable face of your brand.

Events:
Radio has long been famous for its live events, often called remotes or appearances. With the right air talent in attendance, these can be a powerful traffic driver. In addition to live and pre-recorded promotion prior to the event, there is usually an air talent in attendance to do live cut-ins from your event location. Most of the time, the air talent allows the client to be on the radio as well, informing the audience about the event and why they should attend. Like anything else, there's a right way and a wrong way to do these. I

believe if you utilize live remotes, your offer should be limited, unique and valuable to your prospect. Throughout my years in radio, I witnessed hundreds of auto dealers using remotes incorrectly. Their offers were almost always the same from month to month, or they were certainly no different than their direct competitors. The advertisers who went the extra mile to create an offer that was truly exclusive to them were the ones who benefited most from these types of events.

RADIO'S DIRECT COMPETITORS

This book wouldn't be complete without addressing terrestrial radio's direct competitors—satellite radio and internet radio. Here's a brief snapshot of each.

Satellite Radio:

While terrestrial radio is geographically defined, satellite radio can be broadcast across the entire country, and up to 200 miles off-shore in some instances. Among its benefits are a wide variety of programming in virtually every format, national coverage and the fact that most of the stations are commercial-free. Satellite radio makes its money from individual subscribers, who pay to have the service. While there are home and portable options of satellite radio, most listening is done in vehicles.

Internet Radio:

Internet radio options are practically limitless and include Pandora, Spotify, iHeart Radio, iTunes Radio, Slacker and many more. Pandora is currently capturing the lion's share of online listeners, but iTunes Radio has gained impressive ground since its debut in November of 2013. Pandora's monthly unique visitors are approximately 76 million right now (Source: Pandora.com). A new national survey found that the weekly audience for all forms of online radio is now 36% of all Americans age 12 and older (Source: *The Infinite Dial 2014*, Edison Research and Triton Digital). So what does this mean to you? It's an area to watch, for sure, since most users of these platforms must register and provide demographic and psychographic information that is almost impossible to obtain from terrestrial radio listeners. The typical digital advertising options apply, such as rich media and video. Like anything else, compare your audience type, reach and pricing options.

TELEVISION

Traditional television options include broadcast and cable (IPTV options are mentioned in the Video chapter). To begin, I must address a question I receive most often with regard to television, and that's time-shifted viewing, or the ability to record a program and watch it on your own time schedule. The use of DVR (digital video recorders) is increasing, with 34% of

---

142

Americans viewing TV content that is recorded versus live (Source: *Motorola Mobility* study, March 2013). However, as mentioned in the beginning of this chapter, though TV has seen massive audience and viewing shifts, there is still a viable audience for the right price.

BROADCAST TV

Television still has the most marketing appeal among the big three. Remember that broadcast TV is very different from radio, print publications or even cable TV. Consumers do not have favorite 'broadcast TV channels'—they have favorite *programs*. So if you're considering a commercial schedule, targeting by program audience characteristics is critical to achieve results.

BROADCAST TV TIPS

Local News:

Most of the time-shifted TV viewing is done so for sitcoms, dramas, documentaries, etc. When it comes to local news, much of that viewing still takes place live. My advice would be to consider these options first. Purchasing time slots or sponsorships that fall within local news programs can also lend credibility to a *BrandFace*. Look deeper into specific category segments in a news show as well. Many stations have health segments, pet segments, etc., perfect sponsorship opportunities which allow you to share your expertise and be viewed as an authority. There should be opportunities for both advertising and public relations, so make sure to ask about both.

Sports Programming:

Like local news, sports is a category that is most often watched live, whether it's local or national content. TV stations almost always have some type of local sports programming. I've seen creative ties with pizza companies, beer brands, energy drinks and more.

Creative Placement:

One of the most creative forms of ad placement to combat time shifted viewing is to purchase a short (five second) spot right before a program begins. When you record the program, that five second commercial shows right before the program begins to play, meaning the audience can't escape your message. An important part of this placement strategy is the length of the spot. Five seconds is not long enough to bother with the fast forward button, but it's long enough to compliment a branding effort. I wouldn't rely on this strategy alone, but as a supplement to a more visible presence, it's very clever indeed.

Product Placement:

Though product placement is alive and flourishing on the national front (like Ford and Coca Cola with American Idol), I don't believe it has been explored seriously on a local or regional basis. What if a construction company offered to build a new set for a local TV station with a permanent sign on the set which says 'This set a courtesy of' (accompanied by the construction company logo)? Product placement will be very difficult to attain with news departments, but consider the opportunities with local interview shows and sports programs, where the content is a little more lax and less serious. Arrange to have your new energy drink displayed on the anchor's desk.

Category Sponsorships:

TV stations can draw large audiences online for a specific purpose. Lots of stations utilize vertical content (content focused on a specific subject) and sell sponsorships across a specific industry or category. A common one is the healthcare category. Exclusive category sponsorships can be purchased which can position you as the expert in your specific field within the vertical. That sponsorship might include TV promos, presence on the website, online video, search marketing and appearances on their local news or interview shows. Sometimes when a credible media outlet creates a program like this, it can almost appear as an endorsement by the station. Vet these carefully, though, as the content can often be buried in a disorganized media outlet website. If you set your expectations going in, it can be a great program.

CABLE TELEVISION

The ability to target on cable TV is somewhat simpler due to its programming structure. Other than the broadcast channels that you can access through cable, each cable channel or network is largely built on a specific type of audience. For example, Lifetime for Women and E! Entertainment both primarily target adult women, meaning most of the programming on those channels/networks is designed to appeal to that target. Compare that to broadcast TV, with a wide variety of programming targets throughout the day and week, from pre-schoolers to seniors. Cable makes it much easier to drill down into your primary target's interests by channel or network, meaning you can achieve more frequency with one target audience while purchasing volume spots on a single channel. Plus, cable rates generally appear lower than broadcast TV rates. However, when comparing apples to apples, cable subscriber households are not as plentiful as those households who have access to broadcast stations (with or without cable). The only drawback to cable advertising is that there are few, if any, opportunities to gain access to local programming or public relations opportunities. Cable is simply a conduit for the numerous TV channel options. I have recommended cable TV to many clients, and feel it's a cost-efficient vehicle for a *BrandFace*.

TV'S DIRECT COMPETITORS

Like terrestrial radio—broadcast, satellite and cable TV have their own aggressive competitors. The new kid in town, Internet Protocol Television (IPTV), is bringing innovation and excitement to TV viewing. IPTV is, very simply, video delivered to your TV, computer or mobile device via an internet connection. Multiple companies have introduced IPTV streaming devices, the most popular being Roku, Apple TV, Amazon Fire TV and Google Chromecast. In response to this new technology (or perhaps vice versa), brand new content channels have emerged, such as Netflix, Hulu, Amazon and others. These channels are accessible through the streaming devices and offer everything from TV episodes and full series to movies and games. In addition, most offer exclusive, original programming you can't find anywhere else.

While streaming video options like these bring even more consumer choices to the forefront, there are some very interesting marketing options that can arise for a *BrandFace*. For instance, Roku allows you to create your own channel for public viewing. It could mean one more platform for sharing your knowledge and expertise (or perhaps even a comedy to enhance your brand). Look for streaming internet video to continue to steal the thunder from traditional TV options. It's affordable, mobile, allows you to be more selective in your viewing options and offers more choices.

NEWSPAPER

There has been much debate about whether newspaper is dead as a traditional medium. Daily newspapers were the first among the big three to see drastic declines not only in ad revenue but in subscribers. Though newspaper was late in acclimating to the digital shift, daily newspaper websites are usually among the top ranked websites for any local market. They are still viewed as a credible source of content, whether on paper or online.

The most mature of all forms of media, the daily newspaper is continuing to adapt to the digital world even today. Some newspapers are moving to pure online content and some are even shifting to more of a community newspaper role. Community newspapers are generally distributed weekly in most markets, and by smaller geographic regions (such as suburbs). Their main strength is hyper local news and politics (specific to the area in which it's distributed) and high school sports. As mentioned earlier, every platform has pros and cons, and every single one is valuable. Here are some *BrandFace* suggestions for maximum interaction and exposure in newspapers.

NEWSPAPER TIPS

Banner Strip Ads:

Most newspapers sell a banner ad strip across the bottom of various sections of the paper (main section, sports section, etc.). This is a great option for a *BrandFace* because you're guaranteed a fixed position on the section cover, which can portray credibility and create repetition and awareness over time. Putting your image in the banner strip is essential. Remember to utilize QR codes and/or list a web address to move your prospects from offline to online in order to create a more personal connection with you and your company.

Special Sections:

Special sections are topic or content-focused sections that are usually printed once or twice a year, such as a Home & Garden special section in spring and fall, a Financial section right before tax season or a High School Sports section prior to fall sports. Special sections provide excellent contextual advertising opportunities. A tax accountant can feature an ad in the Financial section, a landscaper in the Home & Garden section or an Urgent Care Center in the High School Sports section. These sections provide great opportunities for advertorials as well.

Advertorials:

Advertorials are a mixture of advertising and editorial content. In other words, they are paid ads which are written to appear as editorial articles, educating readers on a specific subject. The only difference is that they must include a disclaimer stating that they are a paid advertisement. These are particularly effective because they allow a *BrandFace* to share expertise in a platform that is still considered by many to be the most credible. Learn more about free editorial opportunities in the chapter on Public Relations.

Post-It Ads:

This type of ad is actually an adhesive ad (the size of a Post-It) which adheres to the front cover of a newspaper. They are designed to promote specific and urgent matters, such as an upcoming event or sale. Think about promoting a one-day sale or the debut of a new product.

Editorial Columns:

As part of my convergence (multi-platform campaigns) experience, I took part in a team effort which positioned a local real estate company as an authority on residential home sales across eight different media outlets. As part of the overall strategy, the owner received their own weekly newspaper column to share real estate insights and tips. This was a win-win situation for the newspaper and the client. However, in order for the newspaper's editor to consider this, you must be non-biased in your approach. In lieu of self-promotion, your article content should be informative and well-written. The credibility this approach brings is far greater than any paid advertising opportunity.

Ron's Message

Although you'll hear a lot of people say that traditional media has been replaced by the internet, I still find traditional options to be some of the most powerful forms of advertising. It's part of the classic term, media mix. And since we utilize a video-heavy approach, TV has been an excellent vehicle for us.

We've advertised in virtually every traditional medium available. I believe each has its own place, time and audience. You just have to experiment and see what works best for your brand, product and message. There is no one-size-fits-all solution. I'm very savvy when it comes to negotiating media contracts. I try to get the most for my money every time, and that means great positioning and frequency. We scrutinize every proposal that is presented, and sometimes we have to say 'no' to reps with whom we've had long term relationships.

Beyond purchasing advertising on traditional media, I've been fortunate to be featured as a basement waterproofing expert on every local TV news show and almost all the morning radio shows in our Central Ohio market, as well. I've also had articles written about me in many print publicatons. Even though there is a line between editorial and sales, I still find that it's easier to be featured as an expert if you're a regular advertiser.

Example Q: Basement Doctor Billboard

Chapter 25:

ONE TO ONE EFFECTIVENESS
OF EMAIL MARKETING

Capturing the contact information of your prospects and customers is considered a major goal of many marketing campaigns. Once that contact information is captured, email marketing is an extremely effective way to get your information in one of the places where many consumers spend a large part of their time online—their inbox. Ninety-one percent of consumers report checking their email at least once a day, and 93% of consumers also get at least one permission-based email daily (Source: ExactTarget, 2013). Email is one of the most personal, one-to-one mediums, not only because it's among the top online activities, but because, with the right approach, your customers will give you permission to send them information via email from you and your company.

As a *BrandFace*, take advantage of this access to their inbox. With such a personal connection, you must treat your email marketing messages just as personal, as though you were standing on their front porch delivering a package they just ordered. The goal is creating relationships.

The first question I usually receive regarding email marketing is how to start and build your list, the million dollar question. The follow-up question is "Can't I just purchase a list?" I never recommend purchasing an email list. I've known clients who have gone this route, and it almost never works in their favor. Assuming the list you purchase is even a valid or current one, those candidates will often opt out because they didn't give you permission to market to them. Besides that, it's against the law. And if your spam email happens to be their first impression of you, it's not a good one. As a *BrandFace*, you'll want to be considerate regarding your communication. It's important that you organically build your list through the proper channels. So let's look at some effective ways to build your database.

DATABASE BUILDING

As you read through the database building options below, remember that you are seeking your prospect's permission to send them communication via email, so each time you execute a registration or sign-up form, it must include an opt-in to receive your e-newsletter or other email communication in order to utilize their contact information for that purpose. Include a link to your company's privacy policy on all opt-in communication. A privacy policy basically states that you will only use their contact information for the purpose intended on the form, and that you (under no circumstances) will share or sell their information. It's another way you demonstrate standing behind the principles of your brand. Here are just a few ways to draw the attention of prospects and entice them to opt in.

VIP Exclusivity:

Email marketing should be about making your customers feel special, making them VIP Insiders. This means that the special offers you make available to them should be exclusive to this group of subscribers. A lot of businesses extend the same offers on multiple platforms, which perplexes me. How do you really know which outlet worked best? And if I can get that offer anywhere, why would I choose to become a subscriber? Consider these subscribers as you would the group of close friends that you invite to your annual holiday party. Give them an insider view, insider offers and a reason to feel special and keep coming back.

Contests:

People love to win things. And contests are one of the quickest ways to build a database of prospects interested in your product or service. It's important to make the prize relevant to doing business! In other words, if you're trying to build a database of people who are rabid Volkswagen fans, don't give away a free TV. It has nothing to do with your brand, and will only produce unqualified leads. Instead, consider giving away free gas and oil changes for a year. This ties in nicely with the brand (VW buyers love to travel, and your service department will have an opportunity to interact with them during their oil change visits). You want to make sure you're generating qualified traffic with people truly interested in your product or service.

Free Trial Offers:

Enticing customers to sample a product or service free not only builds your database but creates a new customer almost every time! Give them a taste of what makes your business great and they'll keep coming back for more.

Free Information:

Informational and educational materials such as e-books and white papers are an excellent way to share your expertise with prospects. Not only can you brand yourself as the expert on a particular topic, but it's an influential tool to bring in the most qualified prospects.

Events:

Events which are open only to your subscribers are an excellent way to make your customers feel special. One art gallery invites their VIP Insiders to a unique event each year showcasing local artists and art pieces available at a discount for one night only. You can also use email marketing to promote live social media events, like Google+ Hangouts, a live webinar or Twitter conversation. An effective call to action might be "Join me live at 7:00 tonight as we tackle the myths comparing auto leasing versus purchasing". It's a great way to be unique and keep the buzz going for the growth of your subscriber list.

Notifications:
Some of you may have signed up to be notified when this book was released. Notifications are a great way to grow your database of super qualified leads. If a new sports apparel line is coming to your store, give subscribers the option to be notified when it arrives, which also qualifies them for a special preview event before the line is made available to the general public. When the latest model mobile phone is set to debut, allow people to be notified when it arrives so they can be the first in line to purchase, and include a free car charger with their purchase. Now, that's VIP treatment!

Partnerships:
One of the quickest ways to build your list is by partnering with another company who has a list that matches your target prospect needs. Do so transparently and ethically, though. If you own a restaurant, and you partner with a local wine company to send a co-branded message to their database, include the reasons for partnering on this offer, and then give their subscribers a compelling reason to opt into your own email marketing database. For instance, offer them a free appetizer on their next visit if they sign up to receive your e-newsletter. In turn, of course, extend a similar offer from your wine partner to your own database. Include a photo of you alongside the owner of the wine company, and maintain your *BrandFace* image. And of course, share the offer on your social media channels, too.

Email Receipts:
One brilliant move that is catching on in the retail industry is the strategy of emailing receipts. When you're at the checkout counter, the cashier will often ask if you'd like a copy of your receipt sent to your email address. Why didn't I think of that? But here's *my* twist! When you send a customer the receipt, include a video message from *you* thanking your customer for the purchase and offering them a free gift (discount or free product/service) if they become a VIP Subscriber. Your video should briefly state the benefits to subscribers as well. Then link to a simple form allowing the customer to sign up. It should be warmly received because they're already a customer, and you've just created another amazing *BrandFace* moment with a personal message. Really, I wish I had thought of emailing receipts.

THE LAW

Below are seven guidelines, para-phrased from the CAN SPAM Act, "a law that sets the rules for commercial email, establishes requirements for commercial messages, gives recipients the right to have you stop emailing them, and spells out tough penalties for violations". (Source: Federal Trade Commission). For a more detailed version of this list, visit www.business.ftc.gov.

No false or misleading header info. The 'from', 'to' and 'reply to' fields as well as your domain name & email address must be accurate. You must identify your business or the person sending the email.

No deceptive subject lines. The subject line must accurately reflect what's in email.

Identify that the message is an ad. This declaration must be clear and conspicuous.

Tell recipients where you're located. Your message must include your valid physical postal address.

Tell recipients how to opt out of receiving future email from you. Your message must include a clear and conspicuous explanation of how to opt out.

Honor opt-out requests promptly. When someone opts out, they must be deleted from your system within 10 days.

You are responsible for complying with the law. Even if you hire another company to handle your email marketing, both of you may be held legally responsible.

RELATIONSHIP BUILDING

I also equate marketing campaigns to relationship courting. First, you develop a perception based on a first impression. If that first impression is positive, you start a conversation to see what you have in common. After that, you date for a while to make sure you're compatible. Finally, steps are taken toward some type of commitment. If you expect to launch an email marketing campaign to a group of people who don't know you well and you are expecting overnight sales, it's like asking someone to marry you on the first date and expecting an engagement. One of my favorite sayings about marketing in general is 'It's a marathon, not a sprint', so keep that in mind as you consider your list building and relationship marketing strategy. Here are nine guidelines to help you turn that first impression into a first date, and work your way toward commitment.

GIVE before you take:
Consider database building like a bank account. You can't take money out until you put some in. Invest in your customer by giving them the things they need: tips & advice, special offers & discounts, helpful articles & links, free trials, educational videos, sneak peeks, etc.

RELEVANT communication they can use:
Sending irrelevant communication is among the top reasons people opt out of an email list. Make sure you send information and communication your customers can use. Take this opportunity to be the quintessential *BrandFace*.

REGULARITY breeds familiarity:
Sending too often is another reason people opt out of a list. Sending too *infrequently* is also among the top reasons people opt out. A general rule of thumb is to send no more than once per week and no less than once per month, but do so consistently, right down to the day of the week and time of day.

REWARD your customer often:
Give back to continue building the relationship. Exclusive offers, events and insider information will make them feel appreciated.

RELATE by listening and responding:
Customers will tell you what they want (and don't want). Listen and respond in a respectful manner. Always go out of your way to make a bad situation good again. And always apologize. Even if it isn't your fault, apologize for your customer's *experience*.

ENGAGE by asking for opinions & testimonials:
After you give, ask for your customer's opinions through surveys and even testimonials. This is invaluable information that allows you to serve them better.

RESPECT your customer's time & opinions:
Our inboxes are full of solicited (and unsolicited) information daily. The key to staying in the 'wanted' loop is not abusing that privilege of communicating one-to-one with your customer. When starting a database of followers, ask for as little contact information as possible. Asking for too much is a turn-off. You haven't earned that yet. And you can always get more information later.

RELATIONSHIP Is the Goal--Close the 'Trust Gap':

Building relationships is the ultimate goal of building any fan base. As your customer gets to know you, and you listen and respond, you are closing the trust gap that will separate you from the pack of 'push' marketers.

ASK for action:

Remember a call to action in your email marketing messages. It doesn't always mean you'll get it, but if you don't ask, you certainly won't. Determine the goal of the campaign each time you send communication. Some goals to consider might be viewing your new video, signing up for your next webinar, following you on Twitter, downloading your e-book or redeeming a coupon.

STATS

You can find numerous email marketing stats just by searching, but I've compiled a few below which focus on consumer behaviors with regard to email subscriptions.

Why People Opt In:

58% Subscribe to receive special offers and discounts from a company
(Source: ExactTarget, 2013)

Why People Opt Out:

69% Unsubscribe because they receive too many emails from the business
56% Unsubscribe because the content is no longer relevant
51% Unsubscribe because the content wasn't what they expected
(Source: Constant Contact, 2013)

Best Days/Times To Send:

In our own experience with email marketing, we find that Mondays and Fridays are generally not the best days for open rates. Tuesday through Thursday prior to noon have proven to bring the most consistency. And a recent study verifies what we have already found. Email open rates are noticeably lower on weekends than on weekdays. (Source: *WhoIsHostingThis* 'Email Deliverablilty 101', 2014)

DESIGN & CUSTOMIZATON
Images:

Your *BrandFace* image should be on every email communication. Those subscribers who have their inbox preview panes set to disable images won't see it unless they enable the images, but you're there with a friendly smile when they do. Remember to use your signature branding images in your email communication as well.

Text in Preview:
Many people do have their preview panes set to disable images, so the first few lines of text need to be very impactful in order to capture the attention of your subscribers. Think of it as a newspaper headline. Put your call to action right at the top. Grab their attention with great copy and they will be excited to enable those images!

Subject Lines:
As a *BrandFace*, it's important that these email messages are coming from you, personally. So use your name in the subject line if possible. If images are disabled, they will still see your name, and you'll achieve a goal of the consistent branding of your name over time.

Socialize:
On all email communication, give options to share on social media. Encourage your prospects to Like it, Share it and Pin it.

Personalize:
When someone subscribes to your email list, direct their submission to a thank you page which features a personal message from you, the *BrandFace*. It can be a written message of genuine thanks with your signature or a link to a video with a thank you message, which re-states the benefits of being a subscriber.

CONTENT
Wondering what to send to your prospects? You'll find a more comprehensive list in the chapter on Content Marketing, but here are a few additional ones customized for email marketing purposes.

Helpful Tips & Advice:
People love great advice that helps them save time or money, or just makes them smarter! Any good email or social media marketer today will tell you that a 'Top 10' list or 'Top 5 Ways' document is like gold. Consumers love reading tips and advice that give them quick & easy answers to their problems.

Limited Time Special Offers:
Special offers and discounts are also a great way to build a database and keep in touch with them, and they're the number one reason people sign up or 'like'. Just remember to limit the time to create urgency!

Product & Service Updates:
To keep your current customer base connected, it's great to periodically remind them of your new product and service offerings. The most loyal customers will appreciate being the first to know, own or participate!

Educational Videos:
Educational videos continue to skyrocket as a means of giving customers and prospects a new and convenient way of learning about a business. Business owners often complain about lack of face time with prospects, and video is the next best thing!

Industry Updates:
At times, industry updates can be critical to customers, like industry laws, for example. What prospects don't know can be an opportunity for a business to build a reputation of helpful expertise. For instance, I worked with a customer to craft a message about the new Lead Paint Law, the EPA's law aimed at protecting children from lead based paint hazards. The new law required contractors and construction professionals that work in pre-1978 housing or child-occupied facilities to follow lead-safe work practice standards. This presented a unique opportunity to update our contractor client's customers regarding this new law. We worked with the client on a campaign site and video about this new law, and at an industry event shortly following the campaign launch, his customers were thanking him for being the *only* contractor to provide this information.

Customer Surveys:
In order to serve your customer effectively, you must know your customer. A carefully tailored customer survey is a fantastic way to learn more about their demographics, lifestyle preferences, shopping habits and more. You can now create simple survey forms with ease in your Google Drive account and send a link to your database.

LIST SEGMENTATION
You may have heard the terms *vertical* and *silo* with regard to marketing. This really just means segmenting your business categories by specialty or niche, or segmenting your audience by needs. In terms of email marketing, you can separate your subscriber lists by customer vs. prospect, type of customer, by the product or service they purchased, etc. Segmenting or separating these lists ensures that your subscribers only receive messages that are targeted to their individual needs. For instance, if you send out an e-postcard alert that a new product is available, you wouldn't want that message to be received by the customers who have already purchased that product. As a *BrandFace*, personalized messaging is more important for your company than the general

messaging sent by other companies. The time you spend on a list segmentation strategy can pay big dividends. Here are some tips and ideas for segmenting your subscribers for maximum return on investment.

Registration Form:
List segmentation not only happens when a customer shifts from one category to another, it starts with your email registration form. If you inquire about the preference of your prospects and customers from the very beginning, it makes for a more personal marketing experience. For instance, we executed a contest registration for an Outdoor Living Makeover promotion via social media. On the contest registration form, the opt-in area stated, "Yes, please send me information and special offers on the products and services I am most interested in. Check all that apply." Underneath, there were eight different checkboxes of interest (Outdoor Fireplaces, Outdoor Kitchens, Pergolas, Hot Tubs, etc.). This strategy allowed the registrant to check only those categories of interest, giving them more control over the experience, and ultimately giving our client more control over future messaging to these prospects.

Customer vs. Prospect:
When someone signs up for your e-newsletter, but has not yet become a customer, they should go into the Prospect list. This means you can send them messaging that is a reflection of still being in the dating stage. If you aren't keen on developing a whole lot of lists, this messaging to prospects can include any of your company's product or service offerings, just keep the email short and the offers compelling so it's easy for them to click on the category of the product or service that intrigues them. Once they become a customer, you can then move them into the silo, which best fits.

Customer Lists:
Once a prospect turns into a customer, it's helpful to put them into a list that defines them according to their purchase or need. For instance, once a customer purchases a vehicle, you can move them into that specific 'purchased' list. That particular list will then receive information and offers from your service department regarding aftermarket options, warranties and vehicle maintenance. You should have a customer list for each service category or product category your business has in order to take full advantage of customized email campaigns.

Events:
When you host events, you may want to send invitations to your entire database or just those customers who may be interested in the event topic. For instance, if you sell real estate, and you're hosting an event to showcase

156

some local investment properties, you'll send invitations to those in your database who have previously expressed an interest in real estate investment.

Ron's Message

We utilize email marketing as consistently as anything else we do. We have multiple email lists that help us to target the different customer types and products they've purchased—or haven't purchased yet. We're diligent about making sure that we have a presence in the inboxes of thousands of people each month. The power of email marketing is that each of the people on our list has opted in. They've given us permission to communicate with them one-to-one. We don't overwhelm them.

It's this kind of regular communication that serves as a consistent reminder that we're the pros, the experts. In our newsletters, we tackle educational topics, charity involvement, staff recognition, upcoming events and more. It's really a condensed publication about what's going on at The Basement Doctor. And, like everything else, my personal brand is woven throughout in order to maintain the connection our customers have come to know and trust.

Example R: House Calls enewsletter
Example S: Thank You email response

Chapter 26:

CREATE AN EXPERIENCE
THROUGH EVENT MARKETING

Events and sponsorships provide unique opportunities for you and your brand to be in front of or associated with a specific target audience. Events can provide very creative options, which can help your business stand out in a meaningful way. There are few opportunities to get face-to-face with your prospects in the way that events can provide. This chapter includes some tips to keep in mind when executing an event or on-site sponsorship, as well as some great ideas to fuel your event fire. Each event should provide a platform to deepen your brand experience. Whether it's an industry event or an event that showcases a specific benefit of your business, consider it an extension of your brand.

TARGETING
A successful event is always more about the quality of the attendees and the experience rather than the quantity. Be selective about your events and sponsorships. Industry-related events can be a powerful source of qualified leads, but take a look at each event case by case. One of my clients was faced with the decision of a large food-related event versus a smaller one. We chose the smaller event because it provided a higher quality experience. It was a paid event (versus the larger free event), and we felt the paying attendees would be more engaging because they cared enough about the subject matter to spend the money. Plus, the smaller event provided our *BrandFace* with more meaningful opportunities to have conversations with prospects, versus being pressured with long lines of people at the larger event, many of whom would come for the free food and raffle prizes. Before I consider an event, I like to make sure that at least sixty-five percent of the audience is within your *super target* range. I define a super target as someone who will not only purchase from you, but will become a repeat customer *and* will spread the word about you and your business to their friends, family and network. It's the triple threat target—Purchase, Repeat, Recommend!

PRESENCE
If you can afford to become a Title Sponsor (with naming rights) or a Presenting Sponsor, it can provide some excellent *BrandFace* opportunities. For instance, you can negotiate to help emcee the event, present a check to the event charity or even do radio and TV interviews as part of your involvement. If you need to be cost-conscious and choose a smaller

participation option, just make sure you jockey for position. Try to secure an area near the main stage or attraction, near the entrance or even near the restrooms. Most people never think about the restroom option, but (especially if you're targeting a female audience) it can be a smart move! We females not only take more trips to the restroom, we take our kids and we sometimes even go in packs! Hey, there's a reason for the stereotype.

CREATE AN EXPERIENCE

Your company's presence at the event should represent what you want people to *feel* about your business or brand. It's about creating a culture that is synonymous with what your customers care about. If you're promoting an organic food delivery service, you'd want your booth to be surrounded in greenery, organic materials and earth tones. You want your visitors to feel healthy when they walk through your area and to think about the positive consequences of making healthy meal choices for their families.

On the flip side, there are times you may want to use the frightful approach to educate your prospects. We recently created a very unique strategy for an annual home show. We were asked by a media company to come up with a strategy, which would provide a sponsor-able section for 'problem areas of the home' which might not be visible to the naked eye.   Termite infestation, mold and mildew, allergens, etc. We created a concept called 'House of Hidden Horrors', which was designed to be adjoining tunnels, each featuring a separate 'hidden horror'. The tunnels would join to make one long drive-through corridor with a display similar to a haunted house. Golf carts would take attendees through the tunnel of the hidden horrors similar to a theme park ride. In the pest control area, crawling roaches, flying termites and slithery rodents would be projected across the floor and sides of the tunnel, as well as in aquariums with magnifying glass. In another area, an overhead water mister would represent the moisture in a basement, with faux painted fabric tunnel sides showing mold and mildew growth on concrete walls. You get the idea. Now, that's an experience! And each section could be sponsored by a different company. As a *BrandFace*, you could serve as the greeter or even drive one of the golf carts!

YOUR PARTICIPATION

Once your *BrandFace* status begins to take root, you'll find that many event attendees will come to your booth or area to ask when *you* will be arriving. Don't disappoint your fans! It's not only a perfect opportunity to engage directly with prospects, it's an excellent place to show that you're just a regular guy or gal who is approachable and willing to answer any questions about your business or their challenges. I'm sure you've heard people make comments like, "I've heard him on the radio and didn't really know what he was like, but you know, he's a really nice guy in person!" That's exactly the response you want, and they will tell everyone they know about their experience meeting *you*. I have three words to keep in mind at events: *Humble Rock Star*. Walk in with the confidence that your knowledge and expertise are unmatched, but put on a genuine smile, and make everyone you meet feel special by taking a few moments to shake their hand, look them in the eye and actually listen to what they're saying. You'll make a fan for life, and isn't that the goal of every *BrandFace*? In addition, visit the booths of others (even competitors) and exchange kind words and smiles. Your competitors will still talk smack about you, but at least they will feel a little guilty doing so.

ACTIVATION
Very often, advertisers are content to allow the 'branding' effect to stand alone. I believe that branding *alone* is not sufficient. Engagement and a call to action of some sort should accompany every branding opportunity, especially at events. Here are a few ideas to help you think creatively about events and sponsorships.

QR Codes:
Use QR codes at larger events (learn more about QR codes in the Mobile Marketing chapter). It's virtually impossible to greet or speak with each attendee at an event, so make sure there are quick and easy ways that you can connect on the next best level—video. Link the QR code to a video about you and your business, or if you have a new product or service, show a video of how it works. It's a great opportunity to educate and add a personal touch when you can't shake every hand.

Fowl Ball:
I'm not certain where this original idea came from, but at one baseball park, whenever a foul ball occurs, someone in the stands gets a free (fowl) chicken sandwich from Chick-Fil-A. I love that idea. It's a creative way to tie into the game, and a perfectly acceptable place to do so, since most Americans eat fast food at least once per week.

Wi-Fi Sponsor:
This idea is really an on-site sponsorship and not event-related, but wouldn't it be great if Starbucks sold a wi-fi sponsorship to Verizon or AT&T? As a customer, you could get your free login code on a wooden coin chip or even a cardboard cup sleeve (with the sponsor's logo) when you make any purchase. In addition, the login page could have a special offer from the sponsor, like 20% off smart phone accessories. Not only would this strategy bring branding and activation opportunities to communications companies, it

would help Starbucks eliminate freeloaders who take up bandwidth and seating but don't buy anything!

Recycling:
Let's continue with the Starbucks on-site sponsorship for a moment. Perhaps a more relatable *BrandFace* opportunity might be for the owner of a local Recycling company. What better way to connect consumers to recycling than having your photo, logo and URL on the disposable, biodegradable cup sleeves in a business known for its environmentally responsible culture? Add a recycling tip to each sleeve and even a QR code that links to a video, which demonstrates how you recycle certain products.

Pet Rock:
Let's say you own a pet store, and you've purchased a booth at an event where people can bring their pets. Consider a photo booth where attendees can pose their pet with musical instrument props (guitar, tambourine or mini drum set) and call it a *Pet Rock* photo! You can send the photo to them via email, which means you get their contact info. Then when you send their Pet Rock photo, it should be set in a pre-designed, snappy looking frame with your small logo in the corner. Let them know you will be posting it on your social media networks and encourage them to do the same (Facebook, Twitter, Pinterest, Instagram). In the follow-up email, include an opt-in to receive news and special offers from your store. It's a win-win-win! And Fido will be looking mighty hip.

Simple Hand-Outs:
Distribute business card-sized announcements at events with a call to action driving people online to a campaign site for more information about a specific offer (contest, gift with purchase, etc.) and include an opt-in on the campaign site for database building. These promo cards are small enough to fit into a pocket or purse (which means they're less likely to be thrown away) and very inexpensive to print.

Demonstration:
I helped to develop a strategy to promote a new service provided by a fire restoration company. They had recently purchased a supersonic cleaning machine that was designed to remove the black smoke, smell and even germs and bacteria from all kinds of products, including delicate antiques, computers and household appliances. After the company invested such a large amount in the machinery, we were brainstorming more ways to utilize it to produce revenue. Naturally, if the machine cleaned smoke and tar from everyday household items so well, it could surely take on lesser tasks, right? Our idea was to partner with local high school football teams and clean their

shoulder pads and helmets. We would have the health department conduct a swab test first to determine the level of bacteria before cleaning, then do a follow-up test. The before and after equipment and test results would be on display at local high school games, along with a brochure listing all the different types of products the machine could clean. Nothing sells better than seeing the results for yourself. And who attends high school football games? Moms, of course! The same moms who wonder why their son's sports equipment is only cleaned at the end of each season (yuck), and who also would love to have industrial (but gentle) cleaning options for items such as blinds, rugs, car seats, stuffed animals and more!

Gratitude:

Last year I attended an amazing event (coincidentally heavily promoted and supported by Ron!) called Victory Canteen, an evening of music, dinner and dancing to honor World War II veterans. It was a touching event. I presented an idea to one of the event supporters, which could add more meaning for the veterans and their families and also provide an excellent *BrandFace* sponsorship opportunity. Consider a *Gratitude Booth*, where attendees can leave a fifteen second 'thank you' video message for the veterans. The videos could be made into one gratitude video collage, and all veterans could receive a copy after the event. Create a nice intro for the video showing photos of the veterans at the event, then launch into the gratitude sound bites. You could hand out business-size promo cards at the event with your YouTube channel address, encouraging people to visit your channel a few days after the event and share the video on their social media networks. Ask for each person's email address so you can send an alert to them once the video is complete and ready to share. It's a great way to follow up the event by posting these on social media for more coverage and even linking to it in a follow-up press release. This is one of those times you don't want to over-do your *BrandFace* presence. Simply having your logo and name associated with the video will be enough, as your presence should not overshadow the real heroes—the veterans. And if you've customized your social media channels properly, your image will be there already.

HOSTING EVENTS

We've listed many benefits events can provide, but one of the drawbacks of participating in someone else's event is lack of control. You don't have complete control of the environment, the decor, the signage, the offers, the food, other participants, etc. In that case—host your own event! It can be very daunting the first year, but if you have the right mindset, it can be extremely profitable. You can start with something as simple as a Customer Appreciation or VIP event. Take the time to reward your existing customers, and encourage them to invite guests (who are sure to become your *new* customers)! It doesn't have to be huge or expensive. Hire some local entertainment (musicians, magicians, balloon artists, etc.) and serve burgers and hot dogs or barbeque. If you're already advertising with a local radio station, ask them to come out with their station van for an hour to help you promote it. Or ask a popular air talent to attend and pay them a talent fee. They'll talk about it on-air and post it on social media. They might even do an on-air interview with you to talk about the event!

EVENT PLANNING CHECKLIST

I get lots of questions about event planning, so I thought I might as well include a helpful checklist for you. This is by no means comprehensive, but it's a great start!

Event Basics:

- Define the target audience for the event.
- Know the purpose of the event and overall goals of the event hosts.
- Is this free for attendees or do they pay?
- How will it be promoted and where? (Ask specifics—how many ads, what time frame, etc.)
- What exactly do you receive as part of your sponsorship/booth?
- Is your sponsorship category exclusive? If so, clearly define category and terms.
- If your particular sponsorship is category exclusive, which competitors can still be involved in the event and at what level? This conversation is critical and should be clearly understood before signing any contracts.
- Which traditional advertising components are included with your sponsorship? (Commercials, promos, appearances, etc.)
- Which digital advertising components are included (Banner ads, landing page, video, etc.)
- Who designs or produces each advertising component?
- What verbiage must be included in these advertising components?
- Which company logo(s) should be included in each advertising component?
- Which *BrandFace* photos should be used and what type or size is needed?

The Display:

- What are exact dimensions of your booth or display area?
- Show basic sketch of booth or area layout.
- Make a list of all materials you will need for the booth.
- Will you need water, electricity or wireless internet access?
- How much time will you have to install the display? And when can you begin installation?
- After the event is over, how much time do you have for disassembly?

Manpower:

- How many people are required to man the booth?
- What hours must the booth be manned and active?
- What days/times can you (*BrandFace*) be expected to attend? Your staff will need to know this to communicate with attendees who wish to meet you in person. Very important!

Public Relations:

- Does the event (or your involvement in the event) have a newsworthy component?
- Are there possible promotional partners you can include in a press release (charities, organizations, etc.)? If so, is there an opportunity for cross-promotion (you send to your list, they send to theirs)?
- Discuss press release components and PR distribution list.
- Assign someone to write the release, distribute and follow up with media to ask for interview opportunities.

Activation:

- What are you doing in terms of activation?
- How are you linking your brand to the event? (Creativity)
- Where are you sending people for more information once they leave the event? (Online destination)
- What is the specific call to action for the attendee?
- Discuss special event offers.
- Discuss any disclaimers for offers.
- Create deadlines for offers.

Promotional Materials

Discuss who creates each, specs for each, print time needed and a deadline for each. Obviously, not all will apply.

- Collateral (brochures, postcards, business cards, magazines, etc.)
- Signage (type & size)
- Radio (spots, promos)
- TV (spots, promos)
- Web video (purpose and message)
- Banner ads (where will they link?)
- Text messaging (purpose and message)
- Social media (graphics & messaging)
- Landing page (call to action)
- Email marketing (where will it link?)

Ron's Message

Events provide a unique opportunity to be face to face with your public in a non-intimidating and personal way.

One of the most unique advertising opportunities that we take advantage of is a partnership with The Original Harlem Globetrotters. I have acted as a player for the opposing team, served as a referee during the game, and even acted as a coach. I'm actually a pretty good shot! This is a fun, family event that helps to build both awareness and excitement for our brand in our local community. It is something that people look forward to each year, and it gets a lot of press and generates a lot of laughs.

I've been involved in golf outings, animal adoption events, parades, local music shows and festivals…you name it. Each year we have a float in (at least two) community 4th of July parades, where we showcase a large inflatable dog in the back of our truck and toss out dog treats honoring our local animal shelters. We get really creative with our events and tie in our charity partners when possible.

At the more traditional Home & Garden Shows, we try to secure the most visible spot on the floor and make it look as though we own the event. We use that opportunity to give advice and answer homeowner concerns and have a little fun. I've even interviewed other home improvement companies to give our customers a broad look at the show from my point of view. The other business owners really appreciate the recognition and awareness, and it positions me as the authority in not just my industry niche, but a home improvement authority overall.

Chapter 27:

BIG SOCIAL little media

Social Media is still an enigma to many in the business world, perhaps with good reason, since it was not initially intended for business. In fact, MySpace, Facebook and other early social media platforms were developed and championed by people who simply wanted a place to connect with other like-minded individuals in a casual, laid back manner. When businesses began to infringe upon these casual conversations, they did so with a lack of understanding that the 'social' part is far more important than the 'media' part. And while many businesses have improved their social media strategies, there are still many more who continue to break the rules.

This chapter focuses on how you as a *BrandFace* can utilize some of the most popular social platforms to communicate casually with your prospects and customers. But first, let's answer the most common question of whether you need social media at all. The answer is yes, you need it. At the very least, social media behaviors are influencing business choices. And whether you like it or not, opinions about your products, services, business and *you* are on display for the world to see, communicated through an intimate network of friends, families, acquaintances and colleagues on social media.

A few years ago one of my clients was giving me push-back about having social media presence. I was preparing for a meeting with them when I ran across a Facebook page started by one of their disgruntled customers titled *[Client Name] Sucks*. Little did they know (until that day) that they already social media presence! They just didn't control it. The moral of this story is that the conversation is taking place with or without you. Wouldn't you rather be involved? Everything you do, every interaction, every transaction, is a potential post. Don't let someone else control your image and communication.

Rather than ask whether you should have a social media presence, perhaps a better question is which platform(s) you should utilize and how you should interact with your fans and followers to get the most impact. This chapter includes some guidelines for interacting on social media, content suggestions and a brief look of the most popular platforms, including ideas for each.

FAN & FOLLOW

Did your parents ever say, "You are who you associate with"? I know mine did, and it's as true in the virtual world as the real world. There are guidelines and manners for social media, which will not only help you grow your prospect base, but will help you manage your reputation as well. When you put your name and face out there, it's even more critical that you maintain the image and perception you desire online. You can learn more about that topic in the Reputation Management chapter.

Who To Fan/Follow:
Start by following people, businesses or organizations you know well or support. This is a simple approach and will result in several people following you back as well. Here are some suggested categories to get started:
- People who are like-minded, such as peers and potential promotional partners
- People/companies in your industry
- People/companies who support you
- People/companies you want to support
- People/companies you admire
- Local government officials (Governor, Mayor, City Managers, Council Members, etc.)
- Local or regional Chambers of Commerce
- Local schools & universities
- Local, regional or national sports teams you support
- Vendors who are important to your brand perception
- Local suburbs, developments & neighborhoods
- Local media outlets
- Local charities and non-profits

Like or Follow Back:
You don't have to return the favor to everyone who likes/follows you. Be as discerning about your social media connections as you are about who you would communicate with in real life, be it personal or business. Common instinct is to follow as many as possible, but choosing who you follow says as much about you and your business as who is following you. Before you follow someone, check their stream or feed for the type of content they post. You'll probably be surprised to find how many people (professional or otherwise) air their dirty laundry or inappropriate language and comments on social media.

Respond to Followers:
Always say thank you to a new fan or follower! Take a moment to publicly acknowledge them and be prompt with your response. Same day response is

ideal. When a recognized *BrandFace* acknowledges a person or company on social media, it carries more weight than you may think. Responding to an individual can make their day!

Showcase Your Personality:
If you have a great sense of humor, use it. If you're an inspirational or motivational person, inspire. If you're passionate about a particular subject, share tips and advice in your own signature way. If you're known for something beyond your business or industry, such as being a chef prior to your current position, share some recipes and ideas in keeping with that persona.

CONTENT
By far the most common question I get with regard to social media is about content. I start by helping my clients break down the various types of content into categories, starting with those which are seasonal in nature. A bicycle shop might share maps to bike trails in the spring and suggestions for performance bikes right before Christmas. Start by looking at what your customers purchase, and when. Beyond that, think about all the things they probably don't know about your product or service, but should. Once we come up with a robust list of content ideas, we map those out on a content calendar. Now your base content is in place. Next, add some promotional ideas (contests, free samples, etc.). Finally, listen and respond. If something newsworthy happens in your industry, share and comment to stay relevant. Here are some content categories to get you started.

Share Expertise:
Sharing your knowledge about a particular industry, category or subject regularly can elevate you to expert status and help you master being the face of your brand. Communicate in a more casual manner versus a selling mode. For example, instead of a direct 'call me, I can sell your home faster' post, a real estate agent might share why it's important to have a Buyer's Agent to represent you in a purchase transaction. That kind of advice doesn't just say 'hire me'. It demonstrates to prospects *why* they should hire you.

Did You Know:
Share historical facts that apply to your industry. A great resource, unusual things, breaking news and trends. Be the first to break the news or declare the trend. One of our clients owns a commercial drapery workshop, which produces drapes, cornices, ottomans and more for the hospitality and retail industry. She's known for her expertise in design and fabric sourcing. In keeping with her image and *BrandFace* strategy, one of our ideas for her was to create an annual Design Trends e-book and to post the trends regularly on

social media.

Opinion:
Contribute your opinion on a subject matter you know well, or even the latest news. If you follow others in your industry, you're bound to see posts from those in your network which capture your attention and entice you to share your opinion. Be steadfast with your opinions, but be kind. No one likes a know-it-all on social media, but everyone appreciates praise or constructive criticism.

Experiences:
Did you buy a new car and have a great experience at the dealership? Have a helpful meeting with someone you admire? Find a new widget or app that saves tons of time? Share insights from your daily life if you feel it will help someone else. Try to link this in some way to your business or point of differentiation to keep brand consistency. If you are a food critic, share your experiences with all types of restaurants, and even some signature dishes you create at home. Or, if you're known for a hobby or craft (beyond your business), share those experiences as well.

Events:
Post about local community events, industry events or events of interest to your followers. When you do, remember to use the event hashtag (ex: #CityCenterConcert) to make it easier for other interested followers to search for it. While you're attending an event, consider sharing your insights live throughout the event so others can experience it through your eyes and ears.

Congratulate:
Post a note of congratulations to a person or business on a recent accomplishment. Recognize your own employees or colleagues for their accomplishments. When a person or business receives an award, launches a new product or service, or demonstrates a good deed, post it. We helped to develop a social media campaign for an HVAC company which recognized students who received good grades and accolades from their teachers. Once teachers nominated students for the award, the public was encouraged to vote for their favorite student on Facebook. This led to positive acknowledgement of area students, hosted by the business. It also boosted social media fans and community awareness for the HVAC company. A win-win situation.

Customer Service:
It's often faster today to get a customer service response via social media rather than by phone or email. This creates an excellent opportunity not only

to showcase great things your customers say about you, but to resolve issues out in the open so fans and followers can see how you handle conflict. Whether you like it or not, your business practices are on display for the world to see. Most reasonable people understand that mistakes will happen. It's how businesses handle those mistakes that can make a lasting impression. One of the most poignant examples of this is a Time Warner sales rep who fell asleep on a customer's couch while watching TV. The customer came home from work to find the rep asleep and captured it on video. The video was uploaded to YouTube and has received hundreds of thousands of views. But that's not the remarkable thing. Until this incident, Comcast did not have a presence on Twitter. One of their employees took it upon himself to launch a Twitter account to interact with disgruntled customers and won the hearts of many.

Favorites:
Social media is a great place to share your favorite places, people and things with your network, and your fans appreciate it! They want to know the best place to get Thai food, or whether the most recent super hero movie was as good as the first. They love it when people share their favorite landmarks, lodging and expeditions. It's just one more way to identify on a more personal, casual level.

COMMON MISTAKES
As mentioned early in this chapter, businesses make mounds of mistakes on social media. American Rifleman is a publication associated with the National Rifle Association. The morning after the infamous shooting at a movie theatre in Aurora, Colorado, their tweet said, "Good morning, shooters. Happy Friday! Weekend plans?" Talk about very bad timing. I'm sure it wasn't intentional. It was probably a post that was placed into their stream within the days or hours preceding the incident, and no one was paying enough attention or had the good sense to remove it. The result? Horrible publicity for the publication and the NRA. But the NRA wasn't the only offender that day. An online clothing store called CelebBoutique noticed that #Aurora was trending on Twitter, and promoted it gleefully with details about their Aurora brand name dress. Clearly, no one bothered to see why #Aurora was actually trending. Beyond the blatantly obvious mistakes, let's look at a few of the more common ones.

Presence Without Purpose:
Far too many businesses have some type of presence on social media, but no real plan or purpose for being there. I believe it is necessary to have a presence, but I do not believe it is necessary to have a presence on *all* channels. Utilize the channels you feel best target your prospects and

customers, and those you know you will utilize well and often as a *BrandFace*.

Timing:
As demonstrated in the Twitter 'mistakes' examples, timing can be everything. Remember when the lights went out during the Super Bowl in New Orleans? The social media geniuses at Oreo tweeted a timely graphic of an Oreo cookie in the dark with text that read, "You can still dunk in the dark". This simple act won a Clio award, and was hailed as the most creative ad of the evening. I can't say enough about monitoring your social accounts and responding accordingly.

Auto-Responders:
I'm not a fan of setting an auto-responder when people follow you. This is often done via Twitter. Take a moment to send a personal thank you to each person who follows you, along with a positive comment about them or their business. Though I realize it's tempting to respond with a generic thank you message that is meant to apply to everyone, it's sterile and impersonal, and most people would appreciate a genuine tweet that mentions them by name. I realize there are some exceptions to this rule. For instance, if you'd like to set an auto-responder with a link to a free gift (like your e-book or white paper), that's great. Just make sure you also follow up with a personal response in addition to that, because your fans and followers will know it's a canned response. And on social media, everyone wants to feel like they have a real connection.

Auto-Following:
Don't schedule an auto-follow. You'll end up following people or companies for which you might not want to be associated! Monitor those manually and decide case by case.

Masquerading:
Don't hire someone else to post for your personal account. You can hire someone to post for your company, but be genuine and disclose their name. Don't allow them to moonlight as you, especially if you are a *BrandFace*! If you choose to have a personal account, interact and respond *personally*.

Complaining:
Warning! Be careful to keep complaints to a minimum, as it can be a turn-off to your followers. When you do complain, try to put a humorous or 'silver lining' spin on it. For instance…"The airline has lost my baggage for the second time in two years…it could be a Full Monty meeting." People are drawn to those who show a little humility and take things in stride.

Socializing Under the Influence:
Don't drink and post. Please. Be responsible and realize that you may post comments that are not appropriate or professional when you are under the influence of alcohol or drugs.

Over-Sharing:
Studies of human conversation have documented that 30–40% of everyday speech is used to relay information to others about one's private experiences or personal relationships (source: Department of Psychology, Harvard University). I know you've seen numerous posts about an impending divorce, graphic details of the birth of a child and cat fights between so-called friends. We're a society of over-sharers. I'll cover this more in the chapter on Reputation Management, but it's vital that you keep the ultra-personal information to yourself, and that your employees do the same. Besides being immature and tacky, there are times when it can even invite legal troubles. Set clear boundaries between your public and private life.

Cursing:
Don't use bad language. It reflects poorly on you and your company. This is true even if you are known to be an edgy personality who sometimes uses colorful language. It still shouldn't be on display for all public to see.

Questionable Content:
Don't post inappropriate jokes or comments. Just as it's sometimes difficult to ascertain the tone in an email, the same is true with social media. What might be humorous or poignant to you may not be as readily understood by your followers.

Arguing or Insulting:
Social media is not the place for arguments or insults, whether directed at an individual or company. Regardless of the reason or even truth behind your insults, it displays a negative image for you. A *BrandFace* should always remain above the fray. Don't participate in negativity, period.

MULTI-PLATFORM POSTING
Busy and looking for ways to streamline your social activity? To help with time management, many marketers use multi-platform posting tools like Hootsuite or Tweetdeck, which integrates Facebook, Twitter and other social platforms. This means you post once, and it populates all your social channels. Each multi-platform posting tool is a little different, so do some research and find the one that works for you.

PLATFORM OVERVIEW

The rest of this chapter is dedicated to recommendations for each of the most popular social media platforms. Since there are numerous sites and tutorials instructing on the practical applications, set-up and tips for using each medium, I'll leave those details up to you to search. Instead, I decided to focus on sharing a mixture of five powerful *BrandFace* ideas and tools to utilize with each platform. You'll find that many of the suggestions can be utilized on several (if not all) of the platforms, as the principles of social media are pretty much the same across the board. Hope you enjoy!

FACEBOOK

Although it is my belief that Facebook has seen its maximum growth potential, it is still the most utilized of all social media outlets at present. For that reason, I almost always recommend that a *BrandFace* have both a personal and company page on Facebook.

Product Launch:

If you've been considering adding a new product or service to your line-up but can't decide which product to launch, ask your Facebook fans! Lays Potato Chips recently did this with our 'Do Us A Flavor' campaign. They solicited consumer ideas for their next chip flavor and received over 3.8 million submissions! Then they narrowed it down to their top three choices and allowed consumers to make the final choice. The winner: Cheesy Garlic Bread potato chips. The best part? They saw a 12% increase in sales. You can use this approach with pizza, burgers, micro brews, you name it. As the *BrandFace*, shoot a short, simple video requesting submissions for your contest and post it. Then make sure to follow up with videos along the way thanking participants for their input and announcing the final winner. Invite the winner to your business for a photo and post that as well. Be involved! This type of promotion draws attention to your brand, gets your customers engaged and ultimately drives traffic to try your new product.

Video Plug-Ins:

Facebook has hundreds of developer apps and plug-ins which allow you to engage with your network beyond your news feed. One I recommend for businesses is a YouTube app, which allows you to integrate your YouTube channel into your company Facebook page. This will allow your network to view your *BrandFace* expertise and entertainment videos without leaving your Facebook page if desired.

Boost Post:

Would you like to make your business Facebook post visible to a wider audience? If you're promoting new valuable content or a new product or service, it might be a great idea. You can do this through paying for promoted posts to appear in news feeds. For example, when you are ready to post from your company page, select 'boost post', then 'people you choose through targeting'. You can choose who will see your post based on their location, age, gender and interests. Boost posts start at five dollars each, and you can expose your message to many more people beyond those currently in your network. When you do this, try to keep your message casual in keeping with the 'social' aspect of social media. These paid posts are seen by many to be intrusive, so do everything you can to keep them light and conversational while at the same time intriguing enough to click.

Offers:
Facebook now allows you to post offers to Facebook users. This can be an amazing tool if used properly. Since I believe social media is much more about giving than receiving, I recommend using this tool to give away an item such as an e-book, white paper or access to premium video content. If you have a brick and mortar store, extend an offer for a free item, an impressive discount or free gift with purchase. Target this offer to just your own fans first to gauge the response, and if it goes well, expand to a larger targeted audience. Just remember the spirit of giving when using this tactic.

App Downloads:
Use Facebook to encourage your fans to download your new mobile app! Create a page dedicated exclusively to an explanation of your app, the benefits to your audience and instructions on downloading. You can even create a Facebook group of people who may have an interest in the app. Extend a special offer for downloading, such as offering the first fifty people who download a free e-book or white paper on a subject matter related to your app.

TWITTER
Twitter is a micro-blogging platform which allows for short posts of communication in 140 characters or less. The brevity of messaging alone is a positive point of differentiation. Twitter's popularity has exploded in recent years, fueled by celebrity use as well as young social media fans, most migrating from Facebook.

Live Tweet Events:
The first recognizable use of Twitter on a larger scale was at South by Southwest music festival, where attendees posted over 60,000 tweets per day. Then on February 23, 2014, Houston's Memorial Hermann Northwest Hospital became the first to live tweet an open heart surgery. When it's not

possible for your fans and followers to be where you are, give them play by play commentary from the sidelines! You can live tweet from conferences and other events as well. First, choose a hashtag (#eventname) and use it at the end of all your tweets. Second, choose the most interesting questions or statements from the event. Don't tweet everything. Think of how a news organization uses promotional sound bites to get the audience to tune in for more. Finally, use the speaker's Twitter handle when you quote them so you give proper credit. You can do this from trade shows, concerts, charity events and more.

#TweetAGift:
Starbucks executed this idea flawlessly in 2013 with their @tweetacoffee campaign. Fans were asked to do three things in order to give a free coffee to one of their social media connections. First, they had to link their Starbucks and Twitter accounts. Second, they tweeted a coffee to a friend using @tweetacoffee. That friend received a $5 gift card from Starbucks. Imagine doing this with a free dessert, a home improvement gift card, free consulting session, sleeve of golf balls, etc.

Use Lists:
Lists are a great tool within the Twitter platform, but there are still some who are unaware it exists. Basically, you can either subscribe to existing lists (similar to groups) or start your own. For instance, you might want to include some of your followers in lists such as *influencers, speakers, mentors* or *customers* to name just a few. This way, you can segment your content as needed to a more specific group, and join in on Twitter conversations with that group on a specific subject matter. You can also view all the lists a specific follower is a member of, and join those lists if you'd like to access some of the people in that same network.

Embed Tweets:
When someone pays you a compliment via Twitter, embed that tweet into your website as a testimonial! It's a great way to feature unique testimonials, and it links back to the source on Twitter so your visitors will realize its authenticity. There is an 'embed tweet' option on every post within your stream. Click on it, grab the code and paste it into your website or blog.

Search for Customers:
My friend Don the Idea Guy is constantly singing the praises of Twitter's search capabilities to find new prospects. Visit search.twitter.com and click on 'advanced search'. Type in your keyword selections, such as 'dog grooming', but be sure to type it into the area indicating 'any of these words', meaning those words can appear anywhere within the post, not necessarily

adjacent to one another. This leaves your search options more open. Remember to select the location so you see relevant posts for potential customers within your area. One search can produce multiple people in your community looking for your products and services *right now*.

LINKEDIN

LinkedIn is the world's largest online professional network, and can be one of your most valuable *BrandFace* tools. It links you to other influential business leaders and potential customers. Depending upon your business, you have the possibility of promoting yourself among your peer group and customer base at the same time. Prior to meeting someone in person for the first time, I do my best to connect with them on LinkedIn. That allows us both to put a face to a name and to learn a little about each other before the meeting. I'm still astonished at the number of people who do not have a photo uploaded to their LinkedIn account, or who have a casual, unprofessional photo that looks like it should be on Facebook instead. LinkedIn is your professional networking representation to the world, so make sure the professional image you wish to portray stands true.

Company Page:

Set up your company page with a great cover photo that represents what you do, and include your image in that (unless your image is the profile image, too). Include concise information about the problems you solve for your customers and what makes your business unique. Use this space to demonstrate your positioning. Ask all your employees to follow the page. Then interact by posting updates to your company page which engage your followers and give them important, usable information. Use powerful images to grab attention. LinkedIn allows Showcase Pages, which are individual pages that can be built to focus on specific company divisions, products or services that you offer.

Slideshare Presentations:

LinkedIn owns Slideshare, a slide presentation platform used for sharing knowledge and expertise. You can now embed Slideshare presentations into your LinkedIn profile page, yet another way to demonstrate your *BrandFace* expertise to your peers and prospects. Your network can view your presentation without leaving the LinkedIn platform. Consider assembling a presentation featuring the questions you are most frequently asked by your customers, along with the answers. You'll find other ideas for presentations in the Slideshare section of this chapter.

Group Participation:

Being an authority on a subject often calls for injecting yourself into conversations. Join reputable groups on LinkedIn and join in the discussion. When doing so, be positive and helpful. Just like any other social media outlet, you will be judged by your interactions with others, and this platform can be more judgmental than others since it's a professional network.

Start Your Own Group:
Can't find a group that focuses specifically on your expertise? Create one! It's easy to do, and you can tap into your entire LinkedIn network and invite them to join and support your group. Consider creating a group based specifically on your point of differentiation. For example, if your business sells green or environmentally friendly roofing products, create a group for people who are concerned about the environment, waste and conservation and establish yourself as a leader among those who can help spread the word about such initiatives. As a byproduct, your business will reap the rewards from people who are like-minded. If you do start your own group, just remember that it's your responsibility to lead it. Be prepared to post content regularly as well as start and comment on discussions.

Recommendations:
Recommendations on LinkedIn carry weight with prospects, customers and peers. It's a great idea to *give* a recommendation either before you ask for one or at the same time. I had great success with recommendation responses by sharing the fact that this book and companion speaking series was about to debut. I asked several people in my network to recommend me for specifics related to my marketing, personal branding and speaking skills. I've found that the more specifics you can give to your connections, the better the chance they will respond quickly. Many times people are just looking for a little help to start the process. When you *give* recommendations, make sure they are authentic and personal. Generic and vague recommendations are boring and do not inspire trust. I'm sure you've seen some of those. They sound like this: "I worked with John for eight years and found him to be a professional in all aspects of his job. He consistently went above and beyond for his customers, and is one of the finest co-workers I've known." On the surface it sounds okay, right? But compare it to this more personalized approach: "Tonya delivered a "TED Talk" like presentation that captivated our 400 business leader audience. Her presentation style engaged participation, delighted with "aha" moments and delivered the message I needed delivered. Tonya is an expert in every way and knows how to move people and organizations from cluttered obscurity to the front line of public awareness." A big thank you to Melissa Kunde, Executive Director of the Portland Area Radio Council at the time of our interaction. Melissa is one of the finest thought-leaders and superb creative minds in the radio industry.

YOUTUBE

YouTube is the world's largest collection of user-generated video. It's also the second largest search engine after Google (and owned by Google). You can create a channel and upload videos for free with lots of flexibility in terms of tagging, advertising, linking, etc. to promote your business videos. There are paid options, which allow for more promotional avenues as well. The main points to know about YouTube are that it's difficult to have your videos stand out amongst millions, so be prepared to promote your channel outside of YouTube (as well as inside options). Here are a few thoughts about getting the most from your YouTube channel. You'll find lots more ideas regarding types of videos and actual set-up of your YouTube channel in the Video chapter, but here are a few bonus ideas!

Product Tutorials:

There are few things more triumphant than finding a YouTube video with a step by step tutorial for installing that faucet you are determined to install by yourself. YouTube to the rescue! Consider creating a tutorial for your products which will allow your customers to feel just as triumphant. It makes you and your business out to be the hero. You can either appear at the beginning of the video as the *BrandFace* or throughout the entire video, sharing your knowledge and expertise as you guide your customers through the process.

Company Tutorials:

One day while meeting with a media client, I asked them why they had so many internal meetings. Every time I tried to reach him, he was headed to or arranging yet another training session for some product or service his reps were selling. I asked him whether he'd ever considered just capturing each of the training sessions on video and storing it on a private YouTube channel that only his employees could access. That way, the company would only need to invest in the video session once and their employees could access the company training on their own time, giving them time throughout the day to actually meet with clients and sell stuff! He loved the idea and they began to build the tutorial channel soon after. Consider this for your company, and make sure to integrate your own image or brief introductory message into each tutorial. Keeping your brand and image at the forefront of your internal communication is just as important as external marketing.

Common Sense Minute:

In 2008, I worked on a video strategy for a statewide political candidate. This candidate was excellent at communicating the common sense aspects of running the government, explaining current issues, etc. It was truly her point of differentiation. And we all know that those who can communicate their thoughts and ideas better are the ones we tend to trust more. We recommended a series of videos called the Common Sense Minute, where she would focus on answering the most frequently asked questions about recent political topics. You can do the same thing as a *BrandFace*. It's one of the most impactful ways to demonstrate authority.

Webinars:

Webinars are a perfect way to connect with consumers on a specific topic, while allowing for flexibility. They can dramatically cut travel costs and allow you to pre-qualify prospects with very little waste. For those who are unable to attend the live webinar, you can easily record it, upload to YouTube and send a link. I was meeting with a non-surgical cosmetic center a few years ago, and they shared the challenge that it was becoming more difficult to get prospects to their office for an open house. I suggested they do webinars instead, which would allow not only for scheduling flexibility but for privacy as well. Many women don't want others to know they're interested in cosmetic procedures. If your business considers privacy an important issue, you have the choice not to disclose the names of attendees with most webinar platforms. Share your webinars on social media and in your email marketing. They're a powerful way to share your knowledge and allow your prospects to join you from the comfort of their own home or office.

Announcements:

Before video platforms like YouTube became so popular, businesses used press releases, press conferences and traditional media to make big announcements. Now, those same announcements can be made on video and distributed among multiple channels. If you hire a new high profile employee, launch a new event, support a new charity or hit a huge milestone for your business, use videos to communicate it. You can segment these into a playlist called 'announcements' or 'company news'.

GOOGLE+

Google+ was launched in 2011 and is Google's version of social media. Google+ allows you to build a network of contacts and even place them into groups called 'circles'. It also allows you to '+1', which is similar to Facebook's 'like'. One of differences between the two is that Facebook is great for connecting with people you already know, while Google+ is great for connecting with people who have like interests (not just those you know). What truly makes Google+ different is a video chat platform called Google Hangouts. It allows you to video chat with up to ten people at once, which even differentiates it from some other video platforms (which require paid memberships to allow for multiple user video conferencing). It allows you to share your screen, record the video conference and upload to YouTube. Pretty robust for a free platform. While registered users of Google+ pale in comparison to Facebook, Twitter and LinkedIn, it's growing in popularity and worthy of consideration due to the Google Hangouts feature, and the simple fact that it's Google.

Interview Others:
Use Google Hangouts (video conferencing capabilities) to interview others, whether it's your peers, your mentors or someone prominent in your community. Interview those people whom your own fans and followers might find interesting. As a *BrandFace*, hosting this type of interaction once again puts you in the spotlight as an authority.

Company Meetings:
I have a client who travels frequently, sometimes up to four days per week. When he's on the road, rather than lose face to face contact with those in his office, we use video conferencing to bridge the gap. This helps him to maintain his position as the leader of his company in a personal way, while allowing him to continue his travel schedule. This would be another perfect use of Google Hangouts because (unlike some other video conferencing platforms), you can have multiple video users at the same time, even on a free account.

Survey Your Customers:
Did you know that you can create customer surveys in Google Drive? It's simple. When you're logged into your Google Drive, just click 'create', choose 'form' and follow the instructions to create a survey. Surveys give you great insight into what your existing customers and prospects think about your business, products or services. Once this form is complete, you can embed the form into a Google+ post and send a link to your database asking for their feedback.

Consulting Revenue:
Since one of the primary goals of a *BrandFace* is to obtain a position of expertise and authority, many are also consultants or have consulting aspirations. Utilize Google Hangouts as a video consulting platform and turn it into a revenue stream. You can offer sessions starting at just 30 minutes, and it's easy to set up a Paypal (or other online payment solution) page on your website to allow your prospects to pay in advance for the session.

Customer Support:
Google+ could be an excellent platform for your customers to communicate with you about support issues. Not only can it accommodate long term

posts, videos, photos, etc. but you can quickly launch a Google Hangout session to have a face to face chat for any issues you feel warrant the more personal form of communication.

PINTEREST
Pinterest is a virtual Bulletin board for photos, graphics and video that allows users to post, find, collect, group and create their own boards, grouped by interests or topic. What makes this platform social is the ability to 'favorite' and pin someone else's content to your own boards, and even comment on them. Pinterest hit 13 million users in under a year, making it one of the fastest growing websites in history. The image-heavy platform is aesthetically pleasing and addictive. Wondering how you can capitalize on Pinterest as a *BrandFace*? Here are a few ideas!

Favorite things:
Your fan base is interested in what *you're* interested in. They love to know your fashion, food and business recommendations. You can create separate boards for each 'favorites' topic or put all your favorites underneath one board. It's just one more way to showcase your personality, which helps to form a stronger connection to your customers.

Share Your Timeline:
Create a board about your company 'story'. Show images that are indicative of milestones in your company. Photos of the day you broke ground on your business, the day your first shipment of products arrived, your 100th customer, your new building addition, your 25th anniversary party, etc. Put these photos in chronological order and put the applicable month and year across the bottom. It's like creating a storybook of your company's timeline and accomplishments.

Book Recommendations:
Due to your expertise in your field and your level of success, people like to know what forms your thoughts and opinions. Share your library. Our libraries say a lot about our individual personalities, motivations and inspirations.

Team Bios:
Create a board for each employee of your business and give your followers a glimpse into the professional and private lives of your entire team. When you or another team member meets a customer for the first time, it will feel as though you already know each other. You can even create 'meet the team' videos and pin those to this board. Familiarity breeds trust, and trust means business. Ask your team members which information they would be willing

to share about themselves and allow each person to be represented in the most favorable light for both themselves and your prospects and customers.

Infographics & Data:
One of the hottest trends today is utilizing infographics to share concepts, structure, flow and data. And Pinterest is full of them! If you think about it, it's almost like using a comic strip to tell a story. This is an excellent way for your business to share great information.

SLIDESHARE
Slideshare is a platform designed to share professional knowledge online. Users upload slide presentations, infographics, PDF's, videos and webinars. Individuals and organizations share knowledge which may be of interest to others who may be seeking the same type of content. With numerous categories like entertainment, technology, careers, business, education and more, the content possibilities are limitless. Once uploaded, the presentations can then be embedded in websites and blogs.

Book Previews:
When I first added the *BrandFace* book preview to my Slideshare account, I was pleasantly surprised to find that it had over 70 views in the first few days—with zero promotion! One of my clients often tells me that there's a 'butt for every seat', meaning there is always a group of people interested in something regardless of the topic.

Expertise:
Slide presentations are generally used to present expertise on a topic, and these presentations are most often delivered in person, such as public speaking opportunities. It would be a shame to let all that expertise go to waste just sitting in a folder on your computer in between speaking sessions. As a *BrandFace*, you'll probably have at least one signature presentation or talk. Consider adding a presentation that at least covers the highlights of your talk to your Slideshare account so the rest of the interested world can see what you have to offer.

Research:
If you've ever tried to research a specific subject matter, you know that search engines can yield literally millions of search returns on any topic. And you find yourself filtering through link after link, only to find bits and pieces of what you're looking for. There are some fantastic research presentations on Slideshare which can cover an entire topic. Use your knowledge and even perhaps your own internal customer surveys to share research that others might be interested in.

Press Kit:
Uploading your press kit to Slideshare is one way to share information about yourself and your expertise as a *BrandFace*. It can easily be embedded into your website or blog; therefore, it can be used multi-purpose to share with both your own site visitors and the enormous network on Slideshare, some of whom may be media outlets seeking expert advice or customers seeking a qualified speaker.

Case Studies:
When it comes to business, nothing speaks success louder than a story backed by stats. In fact, some of the most visited pages on a business website are generally those which show examples and case studies. Case studies can also include customer testimonials, making them even more powerful. Slideshare is the perfect place to share these success stories.

INSTAGRAM
Instagram is a platform which connects people socially through photos and video. Its attributes fall somewhere between Pinterest and Facebook, with most users accessing it via mobile. It gives users the ability to shoot and filter (manipulate) photos and short videos on the fly, making it even more personalized. Instagram's popularity grew so quickly that Facebook acquired them for $1 billion in April of 2012.

Photo of the Day:
Imagine you own a Pet Shop. Showcase one photo each day of one of the animals, and ask people to give you a caption based on that photo. It's a fun, interactive way to utilize this platform simplistically. Use filter options on the photos and create unique looks that practically beg for engagement.

Heroes:
People are naturally interested in the thoughts and opinions of a *BrandFace*. Just as the mentors posting idea mentioned earlier, the people we consider to be our heroes set the tone for our own ambitions. Mentors are people you know and those who have helped in some way to shape your destiny. Heroes can certainly also fall into that category, but some of your heroes may be people you have never met. Consider posting a 'Hero of the Week' photo or video to Instagram, just one creative way to reinforce your brand while humbly giving credit to others.

Events:
Post your event photos and share the excitement and purpose of the event. Think of it as if you're letting your fans into your own backyard BBQ.

Include photos of yourself with other prominent members of the community, and add captions which share the purpose of the event and information about others in the photo.

Instant Makeover:
This particular concept works best if you have a business with lots of before and after photos, such as remodeling, landscaping, non-surgical cosmetic improvements, weight loss, etc. This simple idea can demonstrate how quickly your business can make positive changes, and goes hand in hand with utilizing Instagram in a creative way, both to its image-heavy strengths and the name.

How-To Guides:
Another example of sharing expertise, how-to presentations share step by step information which many Slideshare users are seeking. When I am looking for concise content on a subject, I often visit Slideshare first because I know those presentations are generally assembled with expertise and for a professional purpose.

SNAPCHAT
Snapchat is one of the more recent social platforms on the scene with very unique characteristics. It was designed for a youthful audience who loves to send 'selfies' (photos of themselves) or videos to their friends. But instead of having a photo or video that stays in cyberspace, Snapchat designed functionality which would allow your photo or video to disappear just ten seconds after being opened by its recipient. The trouble is, nothing on the internet actually disappears, and as I write this, Snapchat is under scrutiny due to this very fact. Regardless of the platform's ability to make images disappear, users quickly found that they could screen shot these photos and save them to their mobile devices. To battle this challenge, Snapchat added a feature which would alert the Snapchat sender when the recipient attempted to screen shot the image. And the battle continues. The creativity and brevity of this channel, however, creates some unique marketing opportunities.

Moments in History:
One intriguing way to use Snapchat is to share an image that portrays a monumental 'moment in history'. The brief glimpse into these moments is further signified by Snapchat's brief appearance. If your business has a rich history, you can post these each week or month to share your own history. Or simply showcase your personality by sharing those moments in history which are important to you.

Snap Decisions:
Would you buy it? Imagine a shoe store sending Snapchats of a new pair of shoes each day, along with the question "Would you buy it"? Regardless of whether the recipient answers the largely rhetorical question, the awareness, as they say, is already accomplished. It's a creative way to share new trends and designs and to pique curiosity enough to hopefully drive online or brick and mortar traffic. Also consider this same approach with a restaurant. "Would you order it?"

Announcements:
Snapchat has been used by fashion designers who debut their new clothing lines and musical acts who debut their latest album release. Use the platform to announce your own events, new product offerings, partnerships or expansions.

Landmarks:
Execute a community-driven campaign by promoting local landmarks and interesting facts about each of them via Snapchat. This is an excellent idea for a real estate company who wants to be recognized for their knowledge of the area. Make sure to overlay your logo on the image and come up with a unique name or theme for the promotion, such as 'Interesting Things Happen Here'.

Snap Special:
Happy Hour could be the perfect spot for this idea. Every hour, the drink special would change and a Snapchat would show an image and name of the drink that's on special. It's a fun way of engaging your customers at the bar and promoting specific brands as well. If you're really thinking on your feet, you can get some beverage vendors to sponsor this idea and pay for the exposure!

VINE
Vine is a mobile app (owned by Twitter) which allows you to create short videos with a maximum length of six seconds each. They can be created in sequences of two seconds each and linked together or shot as one continuous, six second video. Each short video plays in a continuous loop and shows up in your Twitter feed. The interface is similar to Instagram, in that you see your friends' Vine videos in your feed on the home page of your app. Though it sounds bizarre on the surface, there are some very innovative ways this platform is being used.

Behind the Scenes:
Let's say you'd like to share some behind the scenes footage of you at an event (concert, charity event, etc.), but you don't want to spend a lot of time doing so or share too many details. Vine videos are an excellent option for sharing, because they allow a brief glimpse into your life and interactions with others.

Teasers:
Think about how TV and radio use sound bites or teasers to get you to stay tuned longer. Do this with Vine videos. Have a new product coming out? A new book release? A big announcement? Sponsoring an event? Share that information in a short video and tweet it to your followers. Sometimes it's the brief content that is intriguing enough to cause your followers to share it with their own networks.

Contests:
Ask customers to video themselves going through a car wash for a chance to win free car washes for a year. Or ask them to send a video of themselves singing your company jingle for a chance to win a gift certificate. The ideas are limitless, and the application is fun.

Demonstration:
General Electric uses Vine brilliantly to share a love for science and technology. They asked followers to submit six second science-based videos and they received over 600 of them. They took the collection and curated them on a Tumblr account (6secondscience.tumblr.com).

The Making Of:
Want to show how your staff makes your new signature pizza in six seconds? Consider a compilation of before, during and after shots for a hair salon (especially during prom season!). Six second card tricks can promote a local casino. Weight training tips, quick tour of an RV, promotion of a ski lodge, etc.

—————————————   **Ron's Message**   —————————————

Social media has revolutionized the way we communicate, both personally and professionally. People ask me all the time, "Do you really get business from social media?" Absolutely, we do. It's a powerful vehicle to inject our already strong brand into our customer's homes, families and network of friends and colleagues. It's an instant connection. People can ask questions and get an almost immediate answer in a non-intimidating and very personal setting.

Whenever I've appeared on the local news, I see an almost instantaneous spike in social media followers, proof that the offline world is so closely connected to the online world. We're very active on Facebook, Twitter, LinkedIn and YouTube to name a few. We only have one or two people handling our accounts, though. I feel the fewer people you have involved, the simpler the act of communicating. Don't underestimate social media as a powerful communication vehicle. People pay attention to the comments of others about your brand, integrity and level of service. And they definitely pay attention when you interact with them on a personal level—brand to consumer, person to person.

Example T: The Basement Doctor Facebook Page

Chapter 28:

MOBILE MARKETING
IN A PORTABLE WORLD

Mobile marketing is defined as communicating or engaging with your prospect or customer in an interactive way through any mobile device. This is the fastest growing segment of marketing! The possibilities are literally limitless, including mobile apps, mobile sites, ads on mobile networks, etc.

OPTIMIZED FOR MOBILE

I know you've visited a site (from your mobile phone) which was difficult to read or navigate due to screen pinching, expanding, scrolling left-to-right and other annoying traits of a website that is *not* optimized for mobile. It's frustrating, right? If your current website is not optimized for mobile, make it a priority. It's easy and relatively inexpensive to build a website with *responsive design*, meaning the site automatically detects the visitor's screen size and adjusts the layout and design accordingly. It means the text, images and buttons are an appropriate size for reading (or clicking) on any device. Before responsive design was widely available, the options were to design multiple sites in various sizes. However, many website templates today are already configured as a responsive design, so save yourself the additional steps!

APP VS. MOBILE SITE

An app is a piece of software that is downloaded to your phone and lives there for easy access at the click of a button.

A mobile site is any website that is accessible from your mobile phone (by browser) which does not require software or downloads to interact.

Most businesses don't really need a mobile app. They simply need a mobile site. Though mobile apps have become increasingly popular, almost 90% of downloaded mobile apps are never opened more than once (source: Mobilewalla, USA Today, 2012). So how do you know whether you need an app? If you're convinced that your app is something your core customer would use at least once per week, and if it includes functionality which is not available via a mobile site, then you should consider an app.
Here are some pros and cons of each:

APP PROS/CONS
Expensive:

An app is usually much more expensive to create than a mobile site. The app industry is booming, and it's becoming more difficult to leverage space on any app store. In addition, the app stores charge fees for storing, publishing, certifying and updating the apps.

Updates:
Apps often have updates, which means the user will be required to download them as necessary. It's an inconvenience if you have lots of apps (especially those you don't use very often).

Flexibility:
An app must have a different version for each mobile platform in order to operate seamlessly within that particular operating system. Apple iPhone, Google Android and Microsoft Windows are the most popular. These platforms also require approval for any apps before they will allow distribution. On a positive note, apps can include functionality (like taking photos) that automatically interacts with your phone for greater convenience (which a mobile site cannot do).

MOBILE SITE PROS/CONS
Inexpensive:
Mobile sites are a great inexpensive alternative to apps, and generally much less expensive. In fact, if you choose a responsive design, there should be no additional expense to have your site adapt to mobile screens of all sizes.

Flexibility:
A mobile site can work on any platform without multiple versions. That means all your content comes from one source, regardless of the platform. And no software downloads or updates are necessary.

Searchable:
Mobile sites can be found by search engines. This allows the search engines to recommend sites with relevant content based on the keywords a visitor is searching via their mobile device. A little known fact is that search engines will actually prioritize a site that is optimized for mobile over a site that performs badly on a mobile device.

TEXT MESSAGING
Text messaging is also referred to as SMS, or short message service. Text messaging campaigns usually start with an external advertising message to a consumer such as "text SUB to 90210 for a $2.00 coupon toward your sub sandwich". The word 'SUB' is known as the keyword. And the five digit code is called the short code. There are several different text messaging

platforms for campaigns, and each have their own dedicated short codes. One such platform is iZigg, which allows you to use the short code 90210, one of the most recognizable and memorable zip codes in the country. When executing a text messaging campaign, the response is initiated by the mobile user. They choose to respond (or not) to your advertising message. Once they respond by typing in the short code and advertised keyword, the text messaging system sends a response to their phone based on your campaign objectives. It could be a link to the coupon, a link to sign up for alerts or an opt-in to receive future notifications about events, specials, new products, etc. The mobile user decides whether to opt in, as the same general rules apply to text messaging as to email marketing. A user who opts in, or gives you permission to continue to market directly to them, is a more qualified prospect. Here are a few ideas to consider for text messaging campaigns:

TEXTING CAMPAIGN IDEAS
Alerts:
Alerts come in many forms, and are one of the most effective ways to gain access to a prospect. For instance, an eye care center or pharmacy can offer to text when your contacts arrive or your prescription is ready. An online store can offer to text when your order is shipped. A vitamin or supplement company can text you when a new product arrives. A pub can text you a reminder every Wednesday night when their happy hour includes premium drinks. The list goes on.

Motivation & Inspiration:
This is a great idea for a church, life coach or any person who is known for their spirituality or ability to motivate. Send a motivational quote or inspiration of the day. It's a great way to stay in front of your customers or congregation throughout the week.

Tours:
Text for a virtual tour of a new home, sports stadium, business or manufacturing facility. Real estate agents can use the keyword 'tour' along with their short code on property signage. Stadiums can even show an insider view of the locker room, which most fans never see. And of course, as the *BrandFace*, you'll be the tour guide!

Personal Video Message:
Text to receive a personal video message from the *BrandFace*. Ideas include a fitness trainer who can share the number one tip for firmer triceps, a personal chef who shares the secret ingredient in his signature dish or an auto dealer who shares the very first look at the brand new Ford model.

Special Offers:

This tactic is most common, and can be a powerful traffic driver if done correctly. Consumers are exposed to an ad or message asking them to text to receive a coupon or offer. The text messaging platform auto-responds with the offer, which the recipient can redeem by showing the offer on their mobile phone at the retail location. Take this strategy one step further, though. When you set the system to auto-respond with the offer, include an opt-in like, "Want more offers? Reply with SAVE to receive future coupons via text". Once the consumer responds they will be added or 'opted in' to receive future offers. Side note: If you're accepting special offers via mobile at your business, make sure your entire staff is aware of the promotion and is trained to enter them properly in the register. Nothing can make an exciting promotion fail faster than poor communication and execution.

MOBILE APP IDEAS

Maps:

A map of your grounds (universities, theme parks or even manufacturing facilities) can be provided to your attendees or visitors to better guide them. Include points of interest and historical significance. This provides an excellent opportunity to use your position as a *BrandFace* to greet and serve as their virtual tour guide!

Events:

If you're hosting an event or trade show, consider an app which would make things more convenient for attendees as well as allowing them to share their experience via social media right within the app. You could display the layout of the event space, event agenda, session topics and speaker information.

Ordering:

If your customers frequently order new products from you, create an app which will allow them to scan the barcode of the products they wish to re-order and place their order from within the app. Include a text alert when their product has been shipped. Finally, give customers the ability to review your product and service.

Sponsor vs. Build:

Instead of taking on the expense of developing your own app, approach companies who already have useful apps and discuss sponsoring or private labeling them. Consider sponsoring a local news or weather app, especially if your business is reliant upon changes in the weather (waterproofing or HVAC). A flashlight app might be a great sponsor-able idea for the home improvement industry. Or consider a calorie counting app if you own a restaurant known for its health-conscious dishes.

QR CODES

A quick response (QR) code is a square set of pixels (similar to a bar code) which, when scanned using a QR reader app via the camera of any smart phone, links to an online destination. The user must download the QR reader app in order to scan the code. Once the code is scanned, the user is automatically linked to a website, landing page, video or other destination for more information about a business, product or service.

In order to scan a QR code with your phone, visit your applications or market area of your phone and search 'QR reader'. Your phone should display several free app options to download. QR codes are used most often on printed materials and signage to fulfill a campaign goal and are an excellent choice for taking offline marketing to online.

There has been much debate about QR codes. Though they have been available for years, the adaption of them by mobile users is still lackluster. I believe that is due to the poor marketing efforts behind the code, not the technology itself. For instance, when mobile users scan QR codes just to find that they link to a website that is not optimized for mobile, that the offer is not sufficient or that the content or purpose isn't relevant, it ruins the experience for all. See some ideas below which should help with these efforts.

QR CODE IDEAS

Chef's Special:
This campaign idea is one of my favorites. Imagine you're sitting in a restaurant, and a table top sign invites you to 'Scan the code for the Chef's Special—*not* available on your menu'. Once the code is scanned, it shows a brief video of the chef explaining and cooking his special signature dish, along with a wine suggestion to compliment the meal! What an excellent way to provide restaurant patrons an exclusive, VIP experience by allowing them to view and order 'off the menu'. Take it one step further, and send the chef out to personally greet each table that orders the Chef's Special.

Instructional:
Recently I replaced the fill valve in my toilet. I've done this at least a dozen times over the years, and thought it would be the usual thirty minute job. However, I realized that the last time our bathroom was remodeled, the contractor installed an entirely different kind of toilet. Unfortunately, it was one which required removing the entire tank (bolts and all) from the toilet in order to replace the guts. You can imagine how thrilled I was, but the thrill

doesn't stop there. The replacement instructions might as well have been written in a foreign language, because I inevitably ended up removing and re-attaching the tank no less than three times before I got it right. Dozens of expletives and two and a half hours later, it was complete. Imagine if that supplier had included a QR code which linked to a simple 'how to' video. That would have saved me time and frustration. Every video, whether instructional, educational or entertaining, is an opportunity for a *BrandFace* to connect in a personal way with consumers!

Testimonial:

A few years ago, we were asked to assist with a video marketing campaign for Tribute Equine Nutrition, a horse feed company. Tribute was being used by some of the finest horse trainers, breeders and riders in the country. As we learned more about the benefits their customers experienced with the feed, we knew testimonials were the right marketing strategy. For almost two years I traveled intermittently with their marketing director to visit Tribute's customers and shoot the testimonial videos. It was fascinating to see that every Tribute customer said the same great things about their feed. We felt it would be a great trickle-down campaign, because if the finest horses in the country were flourishing on this feed, it would certainly be a great choice for any horse farm, no matter the size or type. We generated a QR code for each testimonial video, and the codes were used in Tribute's ads in trade magazines as well as on their feed bags.

LOCATION-BASED MARKETING

Location based marketing is based on mobile geo-fencing (also known as geo-targeting). It allows a business to send text messages to an SMS subscriber within a predetermined proximity of the business. For instance, a coffee shop can set parameters for a campaign that would notify any SMS subscriber within a one mile radius and send them an offer for a free small coffee (with the purchase of a large coffee). These offers can be powerful because they are within close range of the redemption location. Malls have effectively used location based marketing to drive traffic to individual stores and/or to increase purchase levels by extending a special offer through a specific credit card vendor.

Like email marketing, location-based marketing must be permission-based as well. The mobile user must agree to receive text messages from the business by either responding to a text campaign or by filling out an online form and including their mobile number. Once you build a list of consumers who are willing to receive SMS offers and alerts, you can easily see how powerful a location-based campaign can be.

As our mobile experiences continue to get more personalized, our options for advertising will become more targeted and less wasteful. Watch for location-based marketing to gain serious ground as both advertisers and consumers continue to learn and experience the benefits of this technology. It's the next big marketing frontier.

Ron's Message

To start, it's critical that all our websites that are optimized for mobile. We've run ads on mobile apps for local TV stations and large events such as Red, White and Boom (our 4th of July event in downtown Columbus). Though I'm not sure of the return on investment regarding the mobile ads, I will say that we're very aware of the power of mobile marketing today.

It's critical that all websites are optimized for mobile, making it as easy as possible for our customers to learn about us through any and every device and even more importantly, to make their search and navigation really simple when they have a problem.

Let's face it, people don't search for The Basement Doctor's website unless they have a problem they need fixed. And when they do, we want to be certain that they have access to the problem-solution approach we've utilized so well across any device, anywhere.

Example U: WhiteCap Direct Mail Postcard

Chapter 29:

THE POWER OF
POSITIVE PARTNERSHIPS

Partnering with like-minded companies who are seeking the same customers can be a very beneficial and cost-efficient means of marketing. In addition, it can help your campaigns appear larger in scale. You must seek partnerships which are not only beneficial to your customer, but each situation should be crafted with an eye toward a win-win-win situation (for you, your partners and your customers). Here is some sound advice for choosing partners, negotiating the deal and formulating some creative partnership ideas.

CHOOSING THE RIGHT PARTNER

Choose a partner with whom you see eye to eye. Make sure they are as passionate about delivering superb customer service as you are. As a *BrandFace*, your personal reputation is on the line, which means partnership decisions are critical. Schedule a face to face meeting before making your final decision. The non-verbal communication from such a meeting can tell you a lot more than a phone call. Check out their online reviews as well. If you see red flags, approach cautiously. Ask common acquaintances about their business practices and reputation. Vet this partnership as you would any vendor. Once you make a decision to partner, if only for a limited time, the perception of that partnership can have a lasting impact.

FAIR TRADE & WIN-WIN

Any great partnership starts with defining the parameters. Here are some guidelines, which will help you to stay focused on a fair deal for all.

Get It In Writing:

Enter into these partnerships thoughtfully and with clearly defined parameters *in writing*. It amazes me how many things are lost in translation or simply not communicated, which can lead to poor outcomes for you or your customers. If the agreement is in writing, you have a document to help settle any issues that may arise, and both parties feel more protected and confident getting started.

Be Specific:

When you draft your partnership agreement, include what each of you gives and what each receives. Start with the messaging for the promotion. Decide exact verbiage and graphics in order to achieve consistency. Discuss campaign goals, expectations and forms of measurement for each of you. Make it clear that each of you will promote your joint campaign efforts on all your social channels (and name each), how often you will post, and where that post will link. Include information about sending to your email subscribers, when this will take place and how many subscribers you have. You do not need to hand over your subscriber list, but you need to be transparent about the fact that each of you is hoping to gain new opt-in customers from the others' database.

Define a Time Frame:
Clearly define a start and stop time for these opportunities. This move becomes a saving grace if the situation is not working out. No matter how well you know another business owner, complicated situations can arise and you may need to opt out of the partnership or choose to discontinue. Conversely, if it's a raging success, you can always extend the time or decide to repeat the promotion at a later date.

Don't Always Discount:
Price is almost always near the top of the list for consideration when purchasing, but it's *almost never* the number *one* reason people buy. I'm generally against the strategy of discounting. I believe it devalues your company and your products and services, and especially your expertise as a *BrandFace*. Instead of price discounts, utilize point of sale promotions that emphasize the lifestyle of your primary customer. Partnerships are perfect for reinforcing value over price.

CROSS-PROMOTIONAL IDEAS
As a *BrandFace*, you can market cross-promotional partnerships as you would anything else. If you are already a recognized *BrandFace* in your community, you'll be able to be much more selective in your partnership choices due to this recognition. You'll find that parallel partners want to do business with you because it will elevate their own credibility. Ask your partner to join you in videos and photos for collateral materials and social media to support the promotion. A *BrandFace* who is seen as cooperative and friendly to other business owners, benefits even more from this approach. Here are a few different ideas spanning various business categories that I have generated in my work with media and business clients over the years. I hope they get your creative juices flowing!

Home Remodeling:
Partner with an electronics company to provide a home theatre system at an attractive price (or include free installation of the system) with a remodeling contract. A 'gift with purchase' concept can easily tip the scales in your favor

and expose both partners to qualified prospects.

Auto Dealer:
Partner with a local bicycle store to provide a free bike with every hybrid car purchase. Both companies will get a lot of mileage (no pun intended) from promoting fuel efficiency and environmentally friendly options. Take it one step further and have a local Ride Share organization sponsor the promotion as well.

Wine Cellar or Distributor:
Partner with a local restaurant to feature a wine recommendation list paired with their top dishes. Arrange weekly or monthly appearances at the restaurant to do wine tastings and pairings in person. In addition, use table top signage with QR codes which link to the *Chef's Choice Wine and Dine* pairings at the restaurant, with videos describing each meal and wine pairing.

Fitness Club:
Partner with a local stylist and clothing boutique to style and outfit your customers once they reach their ideal weight goal. The end goal of feeling and looking better will keep them coming back.

Bank:
Monitor ribbon-cutting ceremonies through your local Chamber of Commerce to find out when a new business has opened. Partner with a frame shop to frame a dollar bill and present it to the new business owner with a note that says, "Here's to many more of these". Personally sign it and deliver it to the new business owner, along with information about the benefits of your business banking programs.

Mattress Company:
Partner with a local spa to provide a free massage and aromatherapy with the purchase of your top line mattress. Nothing says relaxation like a massage and a comfortable bed!

Jewelry:
Partner with a local maid service or concierge company to promote your new line of watches. Most women have at least one major challenge in common—lack of time! When they purchase a new watch, they receive free maid service, which provides the ultimate gift…*more time for themselves*!

Real Estate:
Research has proven that well staged homes sell faster, so partner with a home staging expert to offer free services for just a few rooms or the entire

home. This type of promotion can tip the scales in your favor when a homeowner is choosing a listing agent.

Utilities:

Energy efficiency is a major selling point and focus for homeowners. Some utilities companies provide deeply discounted efficiency shower heads and programmable thermostats to their customers through a special program. Consider partnering with local home improvement companies to offer those same products to their customers. After all, customers don't think of purchasing shower heads and thermostats from a utilities company, but it's a natural connection with a home improvement company. And if your main mission is to improve energy efficiency in the home, it's a powerful partnership to help you promote your program in more homes with these products.

Home Organization:

If you install home organization units (closets, garage systems, media centers), partner with a professional organizer to offer two free hours of service with every installation. Include the professional organizer's information on your website and in your advertising for a limited time in exchange for a discount on their consultations (or even a specific number of free consultations).

——————————————— **Ron's Message** ———————————————

We've had partnerships of all kinds over the years. Some have been fantastic and others have faltered. We've partnered on various promotional offers with electronics companies who provided home theatre systems, furniture companies who supplied rec room furnishings and even a company that specialized in sports memorabilia from The Ohio State University.

When you align yourself with the right people and companies, it can definitely enhance your brand, especially if those companies are also trusted in the community. My advice is to try it. It never hurts to see what kind of things you can accomplish with like-minded people. As Tonya mentions, you just have to make sure you're on the same page in terms of reputation and trust. And of course, make sure to put your arrangements in writing. That can save a lot of debate and frustration at times. And finally, it must be a win-win situation in order to work. It can't work any other way.

Chapter 30:

THE ART OF
MANAGING YOUR REPUTATION

Have you Googled yourself or your business name lately? You might be surprised to find that a disgruntled customer or former employee has posted a negative comment or review. You might also be shocked at how your online reputation may be affecting you right now in terms of prospects, customers, employees and even potential investors. This book would not be complete without the latest buzzword and initiative in marketing, *reputation management.*

Reputation management can be summed up as influencing, clarifying or recovering the online reputation of an individual or business.   Reputation influence occurs through positive online associations such as reviews, content and public relations activities. The clarification comes into play to make sure that the correct knowledge is shared in order to combat misinformation and enhance perception. Finally, recovery is the stage at which you work to overcome actions or influences that have had a noticeable negative impact.

You've no doubt heard about Target's holiday data breach of 2013. This has impacted not only their day to day business, but their reputation with consumers. In a recent study of females ages 18 and over regarding their level of trust in personal and financial security when making purchases, fewer than half feel secure in purchasing at Target. Compare that to the 75.0% who express confidence in the Amazon.com checkout or even the 60.8% who sense security when paying at Walmart. (Source: Forbes.com, *Shoppers Explain Where Target Went Off Target*, Prosper Insights & Analytics™, May 2014).

Target has definitely been gaining ground in their recent reputation management efforts, but they still have a long way to go to repair this one incident.

This chapter is by no means meant to be an all-inclusive guide for reputation management, especially with regard to reputation recovery. However, I'm sharing a few simple concepts and pro-active steps to help you become more aware and protected.

CUSTOMER REVIEWS
Everything we do online, from social media activities to email communication

to content marketing is on display. And there is no way to stop customers from sharing their opinions, right or wrong. As the old saying goes, we must play with the hand of cards we're dealt. So what can you do to ensure that your reputation as a *BrandFace* remains at the highest standard? Manage it. Communicate, respond and engage. And one of the most effective ways to do that is to solicit positive reviews from happy customers.

Online reviews are critical to consumers today, and even more critical to your business. They're so important that many businesses allow their customers to contribute reviews and feedback (including the negative ones) on their main website. As mentioned in the Social Media chapter, conversations about you are happening online, regardless of whether you approve. So why not inject yourself into those conversations and dispel any misinformation about you and your business? Review sites such as the Yelp, Angie's List, Better Business Bureau, Google+ Local (also known as Google Reviews) and many, many more allow consumers to vent openly about their interactions with your business. Social media platforms can also impact your online perception as people utilize that space as an open review forum. How you choose to engage and respond to online comments and reviews says a lot to prospects about whether they want to do business with you. Learn more about responding to both positive and negative reviews in the 'solutions' area of this chapter.

I could write an entire book on the importance of using your loyal customers as a mouthpiece for your brand. Not only are they the most positive influence on prospective customers, if treated properly, they will provide your greatest source of income—upsell of additional products and services. Gaining a customer's trust initially is the most difficult part. But once that trust is proven, the next sale is as easy as defining their next need. Turn your customers into raving fans and they will *want* to buy more from you. Once they trust you, they will encourage others to do the same.

SOCIAL MEDIA
Your Presence:
First, let's address your own social media presence. There is no dividing line between your company Facebook page and your personal Facebook page in terms of your reputation. If you make the commitment to become a *BrandFace*, be aware that your presence *everywhere* will now be synonymous with your business brand. This means everything you post is on public display. Live by this one simple rule: if it isn't something you'd be proud to share on a huge billboard for your entire hometown to see, don't post it. If it's questionable at all, don't post it.

Employee Presence:

Most of us know by now that companies check out the social media pages of prospective employees prior to and during the interview process, and sometimes the hiring decision is based on that initial perception. But as a *BrandFace*, how do the online activities of employees affect you and your company? Let's face it. You can't control the private lives of your teammates or employees. However, you can definitely limit the impact their online actions may have on an affiliation with your company. I strongly suggest adding a social media guidelines section to your company handbook. There should be clear expectations for all employees, regardless of whether they are responsible for posting on behalf of your company. You should have one set of strict guidelines for those who post on the company's behalf and another set for your employees who list your company as their workplace on their own social media page. As I mentioned, you can't dictate their personal behaviors outside of work, but you can set clear expectations in order to allow them to be a publicized member of your team. If they are willing to abide by those expectations on their personal social media accounts, you thereby give them permission to share that they work for your company as well as link to your company page. If they choose *not* to abide by those guidelines, ask that they simply do not list your company on any social media platforms as their workplace.

SOLUTIONS

Reputation Management firms are often used by larger companies who wish to be *proactive*—or by any size company as a *reactive* measure to a public relations problem. Though all size businesses may benefit from short term outside assistance and guidance in reputation management, most small to medium size companies don't really need to hire an outside company long term. Adhering to some simple proactive measures in a diligent manner will help you put your best face forward and better manage your reputation and perception on SERPs (Search Engine Results Pages).

Content:

Posting knowledgeable and positive content regularly on behalf of you and your company (especially through a company blog) is one of the most effective ways to manage what online visitors perceive. Think of it as though you are the editor of your own magazine. You control the content and image you wish to portray. More meaningful content means more opportunities for online visitors to have positive interactions with your brand. It also means greater potential for positive search returns.

Social Media:

You can influence your reputation on social media with positive content and interaction. Monitor your social platforms at least twice daily to handle any and all customer service comments (good or bad). Most reasonable people will understand that no business—or *BrandFace*—is perfect. They understand that honest mistakes and even bad decisions happen occasionally. The opinions the public forms about you are more related to *how you handle* conflicts rather than the conflicts themselves. This is what makes your position as a *BrandFace* truly influential. Your own personal response and interaction to your social media followers carries a lot of weight, and proper handling of a situation can quickly diffuse any negative fallout.

Public Relations:

Community involvement is a critical part of the *BrandFace* concept, and can be hugely helpful with regard to reputation management. Your positive partnerships, sponsorships and affiliations can gain you invaluable press coverage, which often ends up near the top of search results due to the news organizations that publish the information. Charitable acts and associations are perhaps the most beneficial to your company.

Customer Service:

The very best way to combat negative online comments is to provide superb customer service. There are no shortcuts! As mentioned in the Public Relations chapter, every interaction you have as a *BrandFace* is an opportunity to create a positive brand image. This mentality should be a common thread throughout your entire company.

Respond:

Respond with gratitude when you receive positive reviews. A personal 'thank you' from a *BrandFace* can be extremely impactful. And when you receive negative comments, respond promptly and courteously. First, offer an apology for their experience. Second, offer to set up a personal phone call to resolve the matter. Remember that you are sharing these courteous responses not only for the person who posted the negative review, but even more importantly for the hundreds, even thousands, who will witness how you deal with the situation.

Ask For Reviews:

Asking your current customers and biggest fans for online reviews is one of the best ways to enhance your online reputation. Strike while the iron is hot. When someone pays you a compliment, ask permission to use their comment as a testimonial on your website and social platforms. Offer to include their photo, story and comments in your next blog post. Ask your loyal customers to take a photo with you! You'll find that most people will actually love those ideas, and it turns them into an even bigger fan of you and your business! Plus, there's a good chance they will share the blog post with their social network, exposing your brand to more potential customers.

Alerts:
If you have a Google account, you can monitor online search results when someone searches your name or company name through Google Alerts. Just enter the search term you wish to monitor. You can even set parameters such as notification for a specific type of search, geographic region, and how often you wish to receive the alerts. Google Alerts will send you an email alert when the keyword you are monitoring has popped up on a search return.

——————————   **Ron's Message**   ——————————

Your reputation is everything in this business. What differentiates us is trust. That's the theme. Our Google reviews, testimonial letters, videos...they all talk about honesty and trust, how honest our brand is from the time people call us for advice to the time the crew goes out to service. That's our *customers* telling us that the core of the company is trust.

I've always said that you really don't have a choice when it comes to being honest in business any more. With instant access to the internet and the customer's ability to say what they think of you at any time on review platforms such as Google, Angie's List, Yelp and more, you have to be on your toes. If you're not honest, it will come out. There's just no way to hide it.

Our team does a fantastic job of getting reviews from most customers we service. Our reviews show us at an almost unheard of level of customer satisfaction and we're very proud of that. We try our best to capture video testimonials whenever possible because we realize not only the power of being able to see and hear that customer, but because of the search benefits it brings to our business and our website.

If we do get a bad review, we investigate the situation and try to make it right. And we respond publically.

Remember, as a BrandFace, you are your brand. Your face and name is attached to everything you and your team do. If you operate with complete integrity, you'll have much less to worry about in terms of protecting your reputation.

Chapter 31:

BRANDFACE® ELEMENTS
FOR SUCCESS

I'm a systems, processes and checklist girl. Those things are what provides order amidst chaos, and allows one to excel where others fail. With that in mind, here's a checklist of the materials and elements you may need for your *BrandFace* launch. Some may not apply to you. For example, Pinterest may not be part of your overall strategy, so feel free to exclude elements as necessary. As you assemble these items, however, take special care to stay true to your brand. Everything you do should represent you and your business after careful thought and consideration. Purpose, significance and consistency are key to a successful brand.

PHOTOS
- ☐ Photos of You (at least 6 in various poses)
- ☐ Facebook Profile Photo (personal & business)
- ☐ Twitter Profile Photo (personal & business)
- ☐ LinkedIn Profile Photo (personal & business)
- ☐ YouTube Profile Photo (business)
- ☐ Google+ Profile photo (personal & business)
- ☐ Pinterest Profile photo (personal & business)

DESIGN IMAGES & ELEMENTS
- ☐ Branding Images for Backgrounds (up to 4)
- ☐ Website/Blog Header Design
- ☐ Facebook Cover Art (personal & business)
- ☐ Twitter Cover Art (personal & business)
- ☐ Twitter Background (w/ Photo & Image)
- ☐ YoutTube Cover Art
- ☐ Google+ Cover Art
- ☐ Pinterest Cover Art (personal & business)
- ☐ E-newsletter Header and/or Template

VIDEOS
- ☐ About You
- ☐ Business History

- [ ] Products & Services
- [ ] Events
- [ ] Customer Testimonials

PRESS KIT
- [ ] Pitch Letter
- [ ] Bio (4 lengths)
- [ ] Accomplishments
- [ ] Speaking Topics
- [ ] Book or Speaking Highlights
- [ ] Press Releases
- [ ] Media Coverage
- [ ] 4 Photos (downloadable)
- [ ] Logo Versions (downloadable)

CONTENT
- [ ] Frequently Asked Questions (at least 12)
- [ ] Industry Tips & Advice (at least 12)
- [ ] Misconceptions About Your Industry (at least 5)
- [ ] Articles of Your Specific Expertise (at least 6)
- [ ] Opinion Articles about Recent Events or Hot Topics (at least 6)
- [ ] Customer Testimonials

COLLATERAL
- [ ] Business Cards
- [ ] Brochure, mini-book, mini-magazine or book
- [ ] Presentation (for speaking)
- [ ] Promotional Cards (for speaking)

Chapter 32:

BRANDFACE® CONTINUED

The time has finally come to end [this version] of *BrandFace.* You should know that this book could *literally* never end. Not only are the ideas and resources limitless, but by the time you finish reading this paragraph, another game-changing social media platform or mobile app will have been introduced.

I invite you to join me at BrandFaceStar.com as we continue this journey of creating, sharing and collecting ideas and solutions, which can elevate you to star status in your industry. I encourage you to share your comments, suggestions and success stories throughout your own *BrandFace* journey. It would mean a lot to hear from you.

We truly appreciate the time you have taken to read *BrandFace® for Home Improvement Professionals.* With so much content at your disposal, we consider it an honor to have made the list. Now, put on your *BrandFace* and go forth and conquer.

Email us with questions, comments or ideas!
rgreenbaum@mybasementdoctor.com
tonya@brandfacestar.com

AUTHOR BIO: TONYA

Tonya Eberhart is a Speaker, Author and *Agent to Business Stars*. She grew up in Dawsonville, a small North Georgia town best known for making moonshine and fueling the racing industry.

After she graduated from high school, her wild ambitions landed her a theatre scholarship at a local community college, followed by a move to Tallahassee, Florida to attend the renowned theatre program at Florida State University. But she was soon to discover that she was out of place in the quirky, eccentric world of theatre, so she used her acting skills for a more suitable purpose—vacuum cleaner sales.

While selling vacuums door to door to pay for her education, she happened upon the home of a radio station engineer who recommended her for a sales position, which began an eighteen-year journey in radio.

During this time, Tonya observed business owners who were featured in their own advertising and positioned as local celebrities in the market. She was intrigued by this, and determined to help others achieve that same success. She hand-picked clients whom she felt she could turn into the next radio star, and dragged them into the studio to record their commercials.

Several years and radio stations later, now living in Columbus, Ohio, she has continued to learn and use personal branding skills to bring her clients integrated marketing solutions across multiple platforms. In 2005, she earned the prestigious award of Convergence Salesperson of the Year among over 100 sales reps, and while only working part time.

In 2007, she co-founded Remerge (Marketing Services Group) to consult business owners and traditional media companies on integrated marketing practices. To supplement this effort, Tonya authored an online training platform for media sales professionals called Reboot Campus, where over 750 sales reps received training and certification for Digital Integration Fundamentals.

Tonya has continued to work closely with her business clients on personal branding, which brings us to *BrandFace*, written to help business owners and leaders become the face of their business—and a star in their industry.

Tonya is known for her clever marketing instincts, loyalty and rabid desire to take out your competition. She can tell you what to do…and make you like it. She has developed a great track record of helping her own clients rise to successful levels while utilizing multiple platforms to display their expertise. She's steadfast in her desire to work with those who are truly committed to what it takes to be the face of their brand and an authority in their industry.

AUTHOR BIO: RON

Ron Greenbaum (The Basement Doctor) has more than 30 years of experience in the basement waterproofing and foundation repair industry. He is the co-owner of The Basement Doctor in Columbus, Ohio. He has several licensees who are using his Basement Doctor brand. He is also co-owner of Nash Distribution, a supplier to foundation repair, basement, mold and crawl space contractors across the United States and Canada.

From 1994-1996, Ron served on the ethics committee for the National Association of Waterproofing Contractors for two terms and helped to create the Code of Ethics and Standards of Practice for the basement waterproofing industry in North America.

In 1999, Ron introduced the national trademark, 'The Basement Doctor', and continues to be the face of that trademark, appearing in hundreds of major advertising campaigns for print, radio, television and web. He is recognized nationally as an expert in the waterproofing and foundation repair field, often consulted by leading industry publications ad websites for trusted tips and expert advice on home improvement projects.

In 2009, Ron was asked to participate in The Columbus State College Business Program's Leadership Speaker Series. He spoke to students, college employees and the general public about how leadership is acquired, and what leaders look for when selecting individuals for their company. It was that speech which inspired his book, "25 Things I Believe—The Basement Doctor From the Ground Up".

It is possibly Ron's philanthropic contributions, however, which stand out most. He has supported many charities and community efforts, including Habitat for Humanity, Mid-Ohio Food Bank, Special Olympics, Nationwide Children's Hospital, Wexner Heritage Village, Autism Puzzle, Honor Flight and the Ronald McDonald House to name a few. Ron's love for animals has brought a multi-year partnership with the Capital Area Humane Society in Columbus, and the launch of a local TV program called 'Find A Friend', which promotes pet adoptions and is in partnership with a local NBC-TV affiliate.

His professional accomplishments include being the recipient of a Consumer's Choice Award Winner (multiple years), a Small Business of the Year Award, Better Business Bureau Torch Award Winner, Angie's List Super Service Award Winner, CEO Magazine's '15 Business Superstars', and Smart CEO's 'Top 100 Best Run Companies' Winner.

Ron was born in Cleveland, Ohio. He currently resides in Columbus, Ohio with his wife, Terri. He has two grown daughters (Charli and Betsy).

www.ingramcontent.com/pod-product-compliance
Lightning Source LLC
Chambersburg PA
CBHW072307210326
41519CB00057B/3045